Development Finance
as Institution Building

A research study prepared for the
Enterprise and Co-operative Development Department of the
International Labour Office, Geneva

Development Finance as Institution Building

A New Approach to Poverty-Oriented Banking

Jan Pieter Krahnen
and Reinhard H. Schmidt

Westview Press

BOULDER • SAN FRANCISCO • OXFORD

Published in 1994 in the United States of America by Westview Press, Inc., 5500 Central Avenue, Boulder, Colorado 80301-2877, and in the United Kingdom by Westview Press, 36 Lonsdale Road, Summertown, Oxford OX2 7EW

A CIP catalog record for this book is available from the Library of Congress.
ISBN 0-8133-2457-2

Printed and bound in the United States of America

The paper used in this publication meets the requirements
of the American National Standard for Permanence of Paper
for Printed Library Materials Z39.48-1984.

10   9   8   7   6   5   4   3   2   1

Just say NO ... to money losing credit projects

(J.D. Von Pischke, 1991)

CONTENTS

ACKNOWLEDGEMENTS

The present study is a completely revised version of a research report which we prepared for the Enterprise and Cooperative Development Department of the International Labour Office (ILO). We are extremely grateful for their generous financial support and for the encouragement and insightful comments received from Dr. von Muralt and Dr. Balkenhol and the participants of two workshops held in Geneva. We particularly appreciate the fact that ILO has agreed to publish this study even though its findings and recommendations are clearly at variance with the approach of target-group oriented finance which has been pursued by ILO to date.

The present study differs in several important ways from the original research report. Many sections have been rewritten in such a way that they should now be of interest to a more general audience. Most of the specific references to ILO and the activities of this institution have been eliminated and, consequently, the emphasis on group-related forms of providing credit is not as strong as it was in the original report.

In addition to the above-mentioned ILO staff members, other people have provided valuable support to our research work. In particular, we would like to thank Michael Farbman and Elizabeth Rhyne of US-A.I.D., Maria Otero of ACCION/AITEC, Millard Long, J.D. von Pischke and Sharon Holt of the World Bank, and James Boomgard of GEMINI for providing valuable material and sharing some of their ample experience with us.

Our debt to Interdisziplinäre Projekt Consult (IPC) GmbH in Frankfurt deserves special emphasis. Our views on the importance - and the problems - of institution-building have been shaped in the course of a very close and fruitful collaboration with Claus-Peter Zeitinger and his staff at IPC over the years.

We are particularly grateful to Marion Schnellrieder and Heike Voss for typing the original manuscript, to Saki Papadopoulos for preparing the graphs and the tables, and to Frank W. Best and Stefan C. Fellermann for bringing the manuscript into its present form.

As usual, the sole responsibility for the contents of this study rests with us; none of the persons and institutions that have been kind enough to help us, and in particular neither ILO nor IPC, bears any responsibility for what we have written.

Jan Pieter Krahnen
Reinhard H. Schmidt

FOREWORD

by

Jürgen von Muralt (ILO)

This study was prepared for the ILO by Prof. R. H. Schmidt (University Frankfurt) and Prof. J. Krahnen (University Giessen), working for the consulting firm IPC. The research work was designed and directed by Mr. Balkenhol of the Enterprise and Cooperative Development Department.

The study is to provide a comparative analysis of financial institutions and mechanisms within the context of the ILO's renewed focus on programmes against poverty and in support of the private sector. The study was also to place the interest in specific institutions and approaches to finance in development within its historical context.

In commissioning this study, my department was guided by the belief that it needed advice on the strategic options available for building up sustainable financial intermediaries for the vast majority of the active population in most developing countries who are often cut off from the financial market: the poor, women, small and micro-entrepreneurs and their associations. While it is true that credit and finance are not a cure-for-all, it is also generally recognised that incomes, jobs and businesses cannot be created without suitable financial instruments and institutions. A fresh look at finance is in my view also warranted by the growing emphasis placed on domestic savings mobilisation and by the effects on small bank clients of financial sector reform measures. I firmly believe that this is an area where the potential of member-based financial self-help organizations and networking with the banking industry has not yet been fully tapped.

My department considers this research work the beginning of a continuous and systematic involvement with finance. The study is the first of a series of publications on topics related to enterprise and cooperative finance. In addition, the research work has already helped to shape our new programme, "Poverty-oriented Banking", which is the focus of our involvement with financial sector isssues.

I hope that the research work undertaken by Professors Schmidt and Krahnen will stimulate the debate within the ILO and outside about the relations between poverty alleviation and business creation on the one hand and the financial sector on the other.

The ILO and the authors would like to express their appreciation of the support by the Federal Republic of Germany without whose funding the study would not have been possible.

Jürgen von Muralt is director of the Enterprise and Co-operative Development Department of the International Labour Office

PREFACE

by

Bernd Balkenhol (ILO)

Origin of the Study

A major part of the conceptual and operational work in the ILO and other target-group oriented agencies[1] is characterised by an institution-specific perspective to finance. Sometimes the focus is on savings and credit cooperatives, sometimes on crafts associations having financial functions, sometimes on cooperative banks, but rarely on an intermediary within the context of the financial market, having to compete with other financial institutions and subject to regulations and policies of monetary authorities.

---

[1] For example, the report of a meeting in Bangladesh "Group-based Savings and Credit for the Rural Poor", 1993; or Philippe Egger, Banking for the Rural Poor: Lessons from some Innovative Savings and Credit Schemes, in International Labour Review, Vol. 125 (1986), N° 4, pp. 447-462; or various working papers prepared for the Support Programme for the Urban Informal Sector in Africa, summarised in Carlos Maldonado, Les Mal-aimés de l'Economie Urbaine S'organisent - Leçons d'un programme de l'OIT axé sur la participation au Mali, Rwanda et Togo, International Labour Review, Vol. 127 (1989), N° 1; or a comparative assessment of the performance of guarantee funds and mutual guarantee associations: Bernd Balkenhol, Guaranteeing bank loans to smaller entrepreneurs in West Africa, International Labour Review, Vol. 129 (1990), N° 2; or various documents developed by the Cooperatives Development Programme, for example the background paper on "Non-conventional Forms of Cooperation" prepared for the Meeting of Experts for Cooperatives (November 1968); or Gilbert Renard (ed.), La mobilisation de l'épargne rurale par les institutions de type coopératif (Sectoral Activities Working Paper 5.2 WP.12), 1987; or the documents prepared for the VII. Regional African Conference in Harare 1988.

The recent re–orientation of ILO programmes vis–à–vis the private sector has further helped to move financial sector issues to the centre of attention. To be effective and meaningful, business creation and poverty alleviation need finance. In this context a comprehensive and sectoral approach to finance may give new insights into the relations between banks, non-banks and the informal financial sector. A sectoral approach also helps to better understand and tackle the constraints to savings mobilisation and small scale investment.

Financial Sector Issues of Relevance to the ILO

Finance is complex and diverse. Credit and monetary policies influence market-oriented technical cooperation programmes. Some types of banks are of particular interest to the ILO for different reasons, for example development banks, rural banks, savings banks, cooperative banks, but also guarantee funds for specific target groups. In turn, some ILO activities can have indirect repercussions on the financial sector, for example those supporting financial self–help organizations or informal finance. It is impossible to trace here all links between the financial sector and equity- and poverty–oriented development strategies. For the purposes of this introduction it may suffice to briefly review the most salient issues.

ILO programmes are generally targeted. They are intended to bring the poor, small producers into the mainstream economy and allow them to share the fruits of growth. Targeting is a natural expression of the ILO's social concern, of its commitment to equity. It is part of the ILO's "corporate culture". Of the various doctrines about the role of finance in development, poverty-lending is the one that is most germane to the ILO: it is based on the view that finance means to channel funds to investment opportunities with the highest economic and social return, often by way of innovative non-bank intermediaries like NGOs or self–help organizations. The strengths and limitations of this doctrine are critically examined in Chapter B.

There is a second reason why theory and policy on poverty alleviation and finance merit reassessment. This is the practical experience with funds in ILO technical cooperation projects. Revolving credit schemes and loan guarantee funds are the best known examples. The rationale behind such funds is that in order to have tangible effects on income generation and business creation, there must be some provision for credit and other financial services or some link-up with commercial financial institutions, like banks. In practice, it has been shown that most projects with funds have failed to create sustainable mechanisms for the distribution of small-scale financial services. There is a need to examine more systematically the factors that explain these shortcomings.

It may very well be – this is an implication of Chapter 2 – that targeted training and technical assistance may require targeted financing, but also that targeted financing has rarely, if ever, helped to build up viable financial institutions at the service of the poor and small producers.

Going a step further, one could explore what more could be done to encourage the emergence of mutual and self–help–based financial organizations in developing countries. This is a pressing question particularly in those parts of the world where the banking sector is going through restructuring measures and where financial sector reforms have squeezed out small depositors and bank clients from the formal financial sector.

Another issue relevant to the ILO is the financial sector's large informal segment. While the ILO's concern for and interest in the informal sector is well documented,[2] it is only becoming recently clear that the informal financial sector may hold the key for the informal "real" sector as well as for certain adjustment processes of the banking industry in many developing countries.

Purpose of the Report

The ILO commissioned the study to IPC with three purposes in mind:

- to establish a coherent systematical framework identifying the policy areas and institutions within the financial sector that are of particular relevance for enterprise promotion and income generation;
- to analyse critically the inherent strengths and weaknesses of certain institutions and techniques with regard to their potential to consolidate the creation and growth of small and micro-enterprises and to facilitate poverty-alleviating activities;
- to develop - on basis of this comparative institutional analysis - options for future strategies, taking into consideration the ILO's mandate, its unique comparative advantage as a tripartite, non-financing organisation.

---

[2]   The Dilemma of the Informal Sector, Report of the Director General at the78th Session of the International Labour Conference, 1991; also: Bernd Balkenhol, Savings, credit and the poor: What has the ILO to do with the financial sector? International Labour Review, Vol. 130, 1991, N⁰ 5-6.

Structure of the Report

The study deals with formal and informal financial intermediaries in developing countries. Of the multitude of such intermediaries, five have been selected because of special relevance to the ILO's programmes on enterprise promotion and poverty alleviation. The selection is based on two criteria: "target–group–orientation" and the potential for group-formation and/or associative and cooperative endeavours. These institutions and mechanisms are:

- savings and credit cooperatives, representing the most prevalent type of financial self–help organization; the ILO supports these organizations for their potential to mobilise self-reliance among their members;
- rotating and savings groups, representing different forms of traditional self-help associations with more socio-cultural than financial objectives; the ILO is interested in these endogenous forms because they illustrate the inseparability of financial and non-financial considerations that motivate the poor to organise themselves;
- group lending or joint-liability-based lending is a financial technology that is relevant to the ILO because of the potential bridge function vis-à-vis the banking sector; in fact, the various mechanisms of group lending have in many cases allowed the reduction of transaction costs and share the default risk;
- funds within projects illustrating a quasi-financial institution with important injection of grant or concessionary loan resources; this has become an important facet of the ILO project portfolio;
- postal savings banks, representing a formal financial institution specialised in a limited number of products on a very small scale and characterised, in contrast to most commercial banks, by client proximity.

Directions for Future ILO Work: Poverty–Oriented Banking

The poor need efficient, profitable, well-managed banks. It is not special credit schemes on concessional terms that matter to the vast number of small producers, but a durable relationship and a continuous flow of relatively fairly priced financial services. While banks may not necessarily need the poor, one can say that in some regions of the world some financial institutions would be well advised to develop strategies for small financial services. What is more, there are now several examples of financial institutions catering profitably to the small and micro-business: Grameen, ADEMI, PRODEM, BKK.

The study advances three arguments in support of an institution-building approach in small-scale finance. The first argument is sustainability of the financial intermediary that has been selected for income-generation and/or business creation programmes. Institution-building does not necessarily mean to create a new institution. It can also imply various measures to bring about adjustments between market agents (downgrading, linking, upgrading). The central message of the study is that institution-building should be the guiding principle in the design of projects or programmes where the access to financial services is an issue.

The second message is that financing of and by the poor and of small and micro-entrepreneurs is business - whatever the ultimate social rationale may be. The design and management of such programmes must be also subject to the profitability requirements of the financial intermediary. This entails a scrupulous regard to the pricing of services, the cost of capital, to provisions and operating costs.

The third message is that profitability is not just a question of well-balanced income statement. The internal incentive structure governing relations between an institution's management and its supervisory organs, staff and clients is just as important. The study illustrates this point with an analysis of the incentive and governance structure of savings and credit cooperatives.

A

INTRODUCTION

1. The Issue

The major hypothesis of this study is that the problem posed by the provision of financial services in developing countries is primarily one of incentive-oriented financial institution-building rather than one of the availability of "loanable funds". According to this view, financial institutions are not simply instruments or tools with a fixed behavioural pattern which are geared to the provision of financial services to specified target groups. Rather, financial institutions resemble living organisms that change their behavioural repertoire in accordance with their business opportunities and in response to the resource constraints and other constraints to which they are subject. The interests and incentives of the decisive people in a given institution – i.e. owners, managers, and regulators – shape what might appear to an outside observer to be "the" organizational objective of that institution.

This hypothesis, which is at odds with a large part of the received wisdom in both theoretical and practical work in development finance, has its roots in the new theoretical institutionalism and in information economics. If our view on incentives and organizational behaviour is accepted, it has far-reaching implications for development policy. First and foremost, it would indicate the necessity of a shift in emphasis in development aid in the field of finance, namely toward technical aid in the form of institution-building, and away from financial aid in the form of donor-subsidized loans. Second, it requires a much deeper understanding of the organizational mechanics of financial institutions. The latter is a prerequisite for sound policy prescriptions concerning successful institution-building.

2. The Structure of the Book

On the following pages we will try to fuse essential parts of the modern theoretical, or academic literature on incentives, organization and finance with the first-hand experience in financial institution-building, which we have acquired as consultants.

The body of the study is divided into five chapters. The first three chapters analyse the financial system, with the focus narrowing as we proceed from chapter to chapter. Chapter B takes the most general look and discusses why finance is important for development. As will be shown below, the answer has serious implications for possible assistance strategies for the financial sector in the context of development cooperation. Chapter C deals with informal finance in the context of the financial system. We want to emphasize what specific mechanisms make informal finance function, and where the limitations of informal finance lie. Informality forces the participants in such financial markets to be particularly careful in designing self-enforcement mechanisms. This lesson will be important for the conclusions which are to be presented in Chapters E and F.

Chapter D is devoted to financial institutions. Our proposition is that the strengths and weaknesses of different types of financial institutions have a lot to do with the specific incentive structures which govern the behaviour of the institutions, of the people inside the institutions and of the people with whom the institutions have to deal. Special emphasis will be given to cooperatives, groups, group-lending, etc.

Chapter E covers issues of strategy and emphasizes the aspect of target group orientation: What can be done to design or organize financial institutions (in a broad sense) in such a way that they will be interested in – and capable of – providing financial services on a continuing basis to the relevant target groups, which take in the bulk of the poorer population in developing countries. The concluding chapter summarizes the arguments presented in the preceding chapters and highlights their possible implications for the efforts of donors and implementing institutions to define a strategy for development of the financial sector.

"Finance for development" has become a vast field of expertise and academic research, and, as a result, this study must deal with its subject in a selective manner. The bibliography at the end of the study shows that a great deal of both practical and conceptual work is being done either by the international donor community or in donor-sponsored projects. The preparatory work carried out for this study consisted in part of visits to and extensive discussions with experts in financial development who work either at or for major multilateral donor institutions such as the World

Bank, and national donor institutions such as the U.S. Agency for International Development (US-AID) and the German Agency for Technical Cooperation (GTZ). From these conversations, the authors of this study have gained the impression that the assessments and arguments presented here are largely in line with what the leading experts at the donor organizations and in the consulting community think. However, this is not the whole story: The policies and practical work of these donor institutions are still largely determined by views of development finance which were held in high regard some years ago, but which today no longer represent the most advanced thinking on the subject. And the strategies being pursued by many other institutions are even more outdated.

3. Some Basic Concepts and Definitions

3.1 Finance, the Financial System and Financial Markets

As has already been mentioned, this study concentrates on the financial system and financial markets and institutions. This emphasis is clearly apparent in the review of the history of thinking about finance and development (in Chapter B). In order to avoid misunderstandings, this section will provide definitions of the key terms and endeavour at the same time to make the focus of our discussion clear.

The financial system (or financial sector or financial infrastructure) and financial markets are part of a broader concept of finance. Development has its basis in the decisions and activities of the real or non-financial sectors of the economy. Firms and households have to make decisions of an intertemporal nature which can be classified as saving/investing, financing and risk-management decisions. Thus, it is important for them to have suitable opportunities for saving, financing and risk management. It is the role of the financial system to provide some of these opportunities.

In the material presented here, the following definitions will apply:

- *Finance* encompasses the financial side, i.e. the monetary aspects and the intertemporal-decision aspects of (almost) all economic processes. This includes all activities which involve saving, financing and insuring against financial risks.
- The *financial system* (or financial sector or financial infrastructure) includes all savings and financing opportunities and the financial

institutions which provide savings and financing opportunities, as well as the valid norms and modes of behaviour related to these institutions and their operations.

- *Financial institutions* are establishments such as banks which specialize in such functions as accepting savings deposits and granting credit. Not all providers of savings and financing opportunities are institutions in this sense, and not all financial institutions belong to the formal sector of the economy.
- The term *financial intermediary* is applied to a financial institution when its position between savers and borrowers is to be emphasized.
- *Financial markets* are the markets – i.e. supply, demand and the coordination thereof – for the services provided by financial institutions to the non-financial sectors of the economy.

For a comprehensive analysis of financial markets it would be necessary to investigate both the demand for, and the supply of, financial services. This study is more limited in its scope, as its focus is on the supply side of financial markets. Even if a wide spectrum of financial institutions were included, it is obvious that using this narrow definition, the financial markets would comprise only a portion of finance in its entirety, because not every financial decision of households and enterprises leads directly to a demand for the services of financial institutions. These narrowly defined financial markets are only the tip of an iceberg, and the supply of and demand for the services of *formal* financial institutions, in turn, represent only a part of this tip. Finance itself is the whole iceberg. Of course, the visible tip is not independent of the submerged parts. Financial markets are simultaneously a part and a reflex of finance and the economy. This must not be forgotten if measures are aimed at the promotion of the whole system that makes up what we call "finance", since in most cases only financial markets (Chapter C), and more specifically semi-formal and formal financial institutions (Chapter D), will form the organizational basis for implementing aid programmes and measures.

The relationship between the broad concept of finance in the sense of "financial decisions and processes" and the narrower concept of financial markets is illustrated by Figure 1.

3.2 Types of Financial Institutions

In the context of development aid, one of the central problems is the selection of an institution which can be involved as the project partner. This selection should be undertaken with a view to the project aim and the potential of the institutions under consideration. As this study emphasizes the role of financial institutions, all potential partner institutions which are clearly _not_ financial institutions according to the definition given above will be disregarded in the present context. This would exclude ministries, bank supervisory agencies, professional associations and training institutes, and many others, although they may in fact be very important project partners in reality.

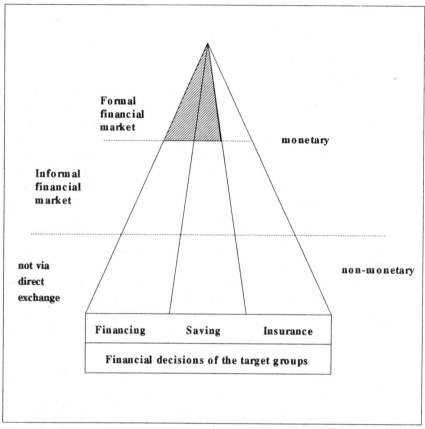

Figure 1: *Finance, financial decisions and financial markets*

Given the overall objective of improving the financial system, those types of financial institutions which exhibit the following four characteristics are most likely to qualify as partners in a development project:

1. They are socially and physically close to the target groups among the poorer population.

2. They have the potential to be viable over the long term.
3. They provide - or are willing and able to start providing - a multiplicity of financial services. In particular, they offer deposit facilities.
4. They are prepared to undergo a certain amount of transformation in the course of the project.

In principle, it would be desirable to analyse in detail which type of financial institution has which potential, how the institutions function, and what operating or organizational characteristics might lend themselves to change. However, it is impossible to discuss all of these aspects in relation to all types of financial institutions which might be relevant for the target population in developing countries.

Therefore, later on in this study we will focus on one class of financial institutions - namely, those institutions which exhibit certain group characteristics - and on one aspect - namely, the governance structure or corporate constitution. However, before embarking on this analysis in Chapter D, we will provide a brief survey of the wide spectrum of financial institutions in this category, presented first in the form of a list, shown in Table 1, followed by a very short commentary on individual types and groups of institutions.This list is sufficient to demonstrate that a perspective which views banks as the only relevant type of institution would be too limited.

Formal-sector financial institutions have obvious advantages over other providers of financial services. However, it is not clear to what extent *commercial banks* can be induced to provide financial services to the target groups in general, and in particular, to lend to them. In the case of *specialized banks* and *development banks*, the key issue is how they could be transformed in such a way that they abandon their policy of subsidized lending. If they do, there may no longer be much to set them apart from all other banks. Development banks still have to find their proper role in a world where financial repression is on the retreat (Schmidt, 1988). They might not find such a role and gradually die.

Savings banks have a considerable potential to transform themselves into efficient target-group-oriented financial institutions. In the case of *postal savings banks*, one of the most difficult questions is how lending can be added to their traditional range of services, which to date covers only deposit business.

Among the semi-formal sector institutions, the *non-bank financial intermediaries* stand apart from the rest. In some countries the legal definition of a bank is rather narrow (as in the U.S.), leaving a great deal of room for "non-bank banks". Often they operate more flexibly and more efficiently than banks, and they might be relevant providers of financial

1.   Formal Sector Institutions
        a)   universal (commercial) banks
        b)   specialized banks
        c)   development banks
        d)   savings banks (POSB)
 	
2.   Semi-formal Sector Institutions
        a)   non-bank financial intermediaries
               ("financieras", insurance companies etc.)
        b)   credit unions
        c)   MP-Cooperatives
        d)   NGOs, DONGOs, GONGOs
        e)   donor-sponsored programmes
        f)   self-help groups (?)
 	
3.   Informal Sector "Institutions"
        a)   money lenders (pure m.l.)
        b)   traders, landlords etc. cum money
               lenders
        c)   self-help groups
               - RoSCAs
               - work groups
               - multi-purpose SHG
        d)   familiy and friends
 	
4.   Mediators
        a)   supporting transactions
        b)   supporting parties to a transaction

Table1: *Providers of financial services*

services to the target groups, which are of interest here. However, the fact that they are indeed like banks but are not subject to banking supervision may lead to problems in terms of depositor protection.

Credit *cooperatives* and multipurpose cooperatives are discussed at length below. As will be shown, their main problem is rooted in their governance structure. Other problems of cooperatives are discussed in Schmidt/Kropp (1987, pp. 84ff). Non-governmental organizations (NGOs), including "donor-organized NGOs" ("DONGOs") and "government-organized NGOs" ("GONGOs"), and other types of donor-sponsored programmes typically exhibit similar governance-related problems: in many cases, it is unclear what system of incentives determines how these institutions - or the financial institutions initiated and run by them - behave over the long term. It would be a worthwhile effort to investigate this issue in depth.

Self-help groups, which take a wide variety of forms and might fall into the categories of semi-formal or informal institutions, have an enormous potential to reach the relevant target groups, but they often exhibit problems in terms of professionalism and efficiency. Support in the form of technical assistance would be helpful in many cases. However, it may be difficult to find a suitable organizational basis from which this support can be provided.

The entire *informal financial sector* will be discussed in Chapter C. It should be added that some providers of financial services, such as money lenders, are more like banks which merely lack the formal status of established financial institutions, while others, namely friends and family, are involved in very informal transactions which employ a more liberal concept of reciprocity than the strict quid pro quo on which banking transactions are based (see also Fig. 1 above).

The concept of *mediators* is one of the innovative ideas that emerged during the phase of "target-group lending" (see Chapter B, third view). Mediators are people or institutions who put themselves between lenders such as banks and poor borrowers and try to establish or support a contact which might otherwise not come about due to access barriers to the financial sector. It would appear that the high expectations which some donor institutions once had about the prospects of undertaking "mediator projects" were largely unfounded (Schmidt, 1985). This generally sceptical assessment, however, does not preclude the possibility that in some countries and in some situations certain types of mediators may be exactly what one would want to support (see e.g. Kropp *et al.*, 1989).

B

FINANCE AND DEVELOPMENT

1. Two Aspects of "Finance"

Among development experts and experts in the field of development aid there seems to be a basic disagreement about two closely interrelated questions: Is finance important for development? And has the topic of finance been given the attention it deserves in thinking about development and in development aid practice? On the one side we find the camp of the traditionalists who claim that the long tradition of "financial assistance" provided to developing countries by multilateral institutions such as the World Bank and by individual donor countries is sufficient evidence that due regard is given to finance. On the other side we find people like Millard Long, the chief of the World Bank's finance division and the leader of the team which authored the 1989 World Development Report (WDR) on "Finance and Development". He thinks that only since a few years the topic of finance has been recognized as important. With reference to the great attention which the 1989 WDR has attracted, he recently told an audience that such a topic would have been unthinkable ten years ago. It would not even have been on a list of 50 potential subjects for the WDR of 1979.

The underlying disagreement is due to the different notions of what the term "finance" means. This term is ambiguous. The most conspicuous activity in the field of finance, the provision of investible funds, contains two apects: One aspect is "capital", i.e. the funds which are being provided, and the other aspect is the "financial system" or the process of providing them and the institutions involved in this process. The question whether due regard is given to "finance" may refer to the aspect of capital or to the aspect of financial system or to both or to their relative weights.

Those wishing to decide whether and how they should support "finance for development" would be well advised to define clearly the sense in which the term "finance" is used, which aspect of finance is deemed important for what reasons and which of the different aspects should be supported. It is the objective of this chapter to describe different views of "finance for development".

In the following section we distinguish four such views and discuss their merits and limitations. They differ most of all with respect to the relative weights given to the aspects "capital" and "financial system".

This discussion may at first glance appear rather theoretical. But this impression is wrong because it can, and will, be shown that these views have a profound impact on how development aid measures which might or should affect large numbers of small firms and households directly or indirectly are conceived and implemented in reality. Indeed, theory has shaped policies to a much larger extent in this field than in many other fields of development aid.

2.   Four Views on the Concept and the Role of "Finance" for Development

2.1   The First View: Finance, Capital Accumulation and Growth

In the years immediately after the second World War, and even as late as the 1970s, development was seen as being basically identical to macro-economic growth. Correspondingly, development theory was treated as applied growth theory. According to this theory growth in real output and income can only be the consequence of growth in factor inputs. Using a simple macro-economic production function and treating the aggregate supply of labour as exogenous, the growth of the input factor "capital" can be regarded as the most important determinant of output (and income) growth. Growth of capital is the result of saving, i.e. of foregoing consumption out of current income. The marginal productivity of capital, measured in terms of output, is treated as a technological issue.

"Underdevelopment" is, in this view, the result of a vicious circle of poverty: poor people – or, as the case may be, poor countries – are poor because their income is so low that they cannot save, and thus cannot invest. Low savings and investment rates lead to low labour productivity and to low income. Poverty leads to the perpetuation, and even the reinforcement, of poverty.

Obviously, this view has much more than a grain of truth to it. There can be no doubt that investment is important for growth. And investment requires that there be something to invest: real resources or the funds to acquire them. This presupposes savings, which may be local or internal savings or foreign or external savings obtained via capital transfer.

It is easy in retrospect to criticize this view of development as growth, and growth as the accumulation of capital, as too narrow and too unsophisticated. Certainly, development is a multi-dimensional process. It has, among other things, to do with growth and distribution. Traditional growth theory tended to disregard distributional issues.

More pertinent to this study's topic is the fact that the traditional view emphasizes finance in the sense of capital and ignores finance in the sense of financial system. Implicitly it is assumed that there is some invisible mechanism which transforms savings (internal as well as external/foreign) into investment and that this transformation is perfect or neutral: The marginal productivity of capital, and therefore the impact on growth is not influenced in any way by the working of the mechanism which mobilizes and allocates savings. It could be an invisible, but perfectly functioning banking system which collects and allocates savings. Or it could be a government bureaucracy which raises taxes and allocates tax revenue to investment ("development") projects. Or it could even be a central bank which creates money and "finances" this by engineering enough inflation to force people into consuming less (Gurley/Shaw, 1960). Whatever mechanism is employed, the relationship between foregone consumption and growth would be the same, i.e. it would be determined by the technological laws which are implicit in the macroeconomic production function.

The implications of the traditional view for development aid are straightforward: If capital leads to growth and if local incomes are so low that they cannot lead to local savings, then foreign savings have to substitute local savings and close the "savings gap". But the flow of foreign funds from industrialized to developing countries is in fact a flow of real resources and it is only a matter of convenience that foreign aid in the framework of "financial cooperation" takes on monetary form for a short time: As the foreign aid funds serve to fill a gap of real resources, they can only be used to pay for the foreign-exchange component of development projects. This means that the foreign exchange flows back to the industrialized donor or, as the case may be, lender countries in order to be exchanged for goods such as machinery.

That is why the development-aid policy of the 1950s and 1960s consisted of real assets-transfers to the developing countries. Financing large projects was, at that time, believed to lead to positive linkage effects, growing employment, and a more equitable distribution of wealth. It was convenient to believe in "trickle-down" because this saved the donors from the industrial countries the trouble of evaluating the economic merits of anything but the biggest projects.

There was, though, one aspect of finance in the sense of "financial system". Except in the case of the very biggest projects, a mechanism was needed which would distribute the foreign funds to local projects, if large-scale measures were to be supported. It was believed that this should be done by local institutions. But there were no such institutions. Existing banks in most developing countries were not equipped to appraise technically sophisticated medium- and long-term projects. Thus, in addition to the gap in terms of savings capital, there was also an institutions gap. Development finance corporations (DFCs) were established to fill this gap, and they received foreign financing to fill the resource or savings gap.

Economically speaking, these development finance corporations were not banks. They were just administrative entities devised to distribute foreign funds. They would not take deposits, nor provide liquidity or transformation of terms to maturity, lot sizes or risks, and they also did not bear the bulk of the risks generated by their activities. So the undeniable fact that in addition to funds institutional innovations were exported to the developing world does not change the general picture: According to the traditional view, "finance" in fact consisted of just the transfer of real resources.

The traditional view is not only too narrow, it is also somewhat inconsistent with empirical facts: The relationship between capital input, as measured by savings and/or real investment, and economic growth is less clear than one would expect on the basis of growth theory. Though savings/investments can explain economic growth to some extent there are many low growth countries with high savings or investment rates, as well as countries with moderate savings/investments which grow at very high rates (World Bank, 1989, p. 39). It seems that another factor is missing in the explanation of growth. As we shall see later on, the missing factor would represent the quality of the financial system and its capacity to allocate investible funds and to monitor their use.

2.2 The Second View: Financing Specific Target Groups

The mechanistic view underlying the traditional approach, and the optimistic outlook connected with it, were being questioned in the 1970s when world events and a general shift in economic policies made themselves felt. The infusion of (foreign) capital into big development projects had rarely contributed to GNP growth, and, indeed, in most cases it had even led to a deterioration in the economic and social situation of the majority of the people in the developing countries. Instead of the linkage effects which had been hoped for, backwash effects tended to prevail, inducing dualism and reinforcing poverty, unemployment and migration.

Donor policy reacted by changing the general orientation and strategy at least at the level of the relevant rhetoric and some of the specific methods of development aid. After "the end of trickle–down", development aid policy began to be regarded as worldwide social policy, aiming at income generation, poverty alleviation, employment creation and similar objectives. The poorer strata were "promoted" to the status of preferred target groups. Concomitant with the change of objectives was a change of perspective: The traditional general perspective of looking at the entire economy was – at least to some extent – replaced by a perspective which would focus on specific target groups such as commercial farmers, smallholders, small entrepreneurs, etc., while at the same time the professional perspective of the economists was being replaced by a social–worker perspective. Since the belief in an economic mechanism which would connect developments in different economic sectors was being questioned and since the dualism of the entire economy of developing countries was accepted as an established fact, the understanding of "finance" and the role of "finance" for development may have been challenged and the thrust of finance–related development policy may have been reassessed drastically. Was this the case?

The basic understanding of "finance" remained the same as before. Finance was still primarily understood as providing capital (in the form of credit) to those who would be able to use it optimally. Only the recipients and users of capital and the standards for judging what constitutes "optimal use" were different.

Farmers and small business instead of big business and public institutions became the preferred target groups. There can be no doubt that development on a micro–level also presupposes investment, and that investment has to be "financed", i.e. investible funds have to be forthcoming from somewhere. Although the new target groups may have different types of investment opportunities and may require more than credit as an input factor, credit was believed to be the bottleneck. Empirical investigations based on simply asking people what their most urgent ("felt") needs were lent support to this conviction. It is worth noting that at that time, i.e. in the 1970s and into the '80s, development experts did not really care whether there was a *demand* for credit on the part of the intended recipients. Rather, in line with the philosophy of supply–leading finance (Patrick, 1966), they emphasized the *need*: Credit (capital) was needed because it would generate, as it was assumed, a positive development impact.

This more social orientation also led to new standards of evaluation such as the "economic" (i.e. social) instead of "financial" (i.e. private) rate of return. Seen by itself, this change of standards reflects the growing mistrust in the market mechanism. The change of standards is still more pronounced where the "impact" in terms of health, employment, education etc., on the target groups was emphasized. Whatever it may refer to in detail, it is most likely that the criterion of impact will be at variance with the criterion of profitability. This had an important consequence: The provision of credit (capital) to specific target groups became a public policy issue. It was felt that farmers, business people and others should be induced to use capital (and other inputs) in order to "produce" employment, income, a better food supply, etc. Demand was neither sufficient nor necessary as an indicator of need.

This is the reason why finance in the sense of financial system received more attention under the second view than under the traditional or first view: it was the problem of the development planners to bring credit (capital) to those who would use it to achieve an optimal impact from a public–policy standpoint. The planners were looking for methods of distributing credit (capital), and quite naturally asked whether the banking system would be willing and able to play such a role. Generally speaking, existing banks were found to be unwilling and unsuited to act as conduits for capital which would come from abroad, from the government or the central bank. This was no surprise: How could banks expect to do profitable banking business with "clients" who might not even demand the banking services which they supposedly needed?

This led to the quest for other methods, instruments and institutions. Specialised development banks for agriculture, (small) industry and housing were set up. The underlying belief was that they might be effective in reaching target groups and, in the final analysis, in producing an impact. However, efficiency in performing these development functions was not a high–ranking concern. There were several reasons for this. A very important one was the conviction that this type of development banking could never be profitable in the first place: The recipients, the target groups, were poor; their businesses were risky; and, above all, it was part of the concept that they had to be lured into taking out loans by charging highly subsidized interest rates. Therefore it was believed that the development banks needed more than funds for onlending; they also needed subsidies to operate and technical assistance for themselves and to pass on to their customers.

It turned out that the government–owned and donor–financed specialized development banks were not particularly effective and at the same time very inefficient. The failure of the agricultural development banks in developing countries is very well documented in the literature (see Von Pischke *et al.*, 1983 and Adams *et al.*, 1984). In the case of banking for small and medium–scale enterprises and banking for housing, the situation is more or less the same (Levitsky, 1986).

There were basically two reactions to the failure of this policy. One consisted of blaming the fact that the partner institutions were too much like banks, as well as the involvement of governments in these institutions and in the entire process, for the ineffectiveness and inefficiency. This criticism led to major innovations concerning the mechanisms, institutions, and partners: Non–banks and non–governmental organisations were employed by foreign donors to "really" reach the target groups, to allocate capital and to monitor its use and eventual repayment. This strategy of poverty and/or target group–oriented lending, which is still being pursued in many ongoing projects, has transformed development aid practice profoundly and produced many valuable insights into the problems that must be overcome if one is to lend successfully to target groups which are normally not clients of banks.[1]

But the strategy of using unconventional channels for bringing credit to target groups has its drawbacks, too. Most important among them is the fact that the institutions which have been, and still are, employed are rarely able to become stable and profitable providers of capital. Their operations are in most cases extremely costly so that it is virtually impossible for them to have a lasting effect and to operate on a large scale. It is gratifying to know that with much technical assistance and heavy subsidies at least some of the poor people in developing countries can be reached, but in view of the huge number of farmers and business people who have no access to the banking system, all the NGO–based activities and other similar efforts and experiments are only a drop in the bucket.

In summary, it can be said that the concept of finance used in the target–group–oriented approach is only somewhat wider than that used in the traditional approach: On the one hand new institutions such as NGOs and cooperatives, and new methods such as group financing, have been adopted and tried. From the perspective of donors, the understanding of "finance" has clearly been broadened and the dimension of "financial system" has received some of the emphasis which it deserves. But on the other hand the view of what this system does and what its role for development could be, is as narrow as before: Channeling funds in order to provide credit/capital as an input to production in order to fill a gap

---

[1] A large number of early insights and innovative strategies undertaken in this spirit of poverty-oriented lending are documented in Farbman (1981) and Ashe (1985).

which was unquestioningly assumed to exist everywhere in the developing world and which was believed to be the main impediment to broad based, socially balanced growth and development.

The second reaction to the widespread failure of the specialized development banks was not to go one more step in the same direction, but to reverse the direction and to look much more generally at the financial system and its functions. This will be discussed in the next section as the third view.

2.3 The Third View: Financial System Development

General outline

The two views which have been discussed above are like quite dissimilar brothers from the same family. The advocates of each approach strongly disagree with each other not only as regards their basic concepts of development and their confidence in the merits of big projects, but also in terms of their concern for the poor. But they share the view that "finance" is just providing credit; that credit is all the poor people (or poor countries) need; and that apart from its function of channeling credit/capital to users, the financial system does not matter for development. Some economists even believed that the financial system is detrimental to economic growth since it is a major source of instability and since it attracts funds which would thus be withheld from real investment.

The financial system was used as an instrument, and it was misused (Von Pischke *et al.*, 1983). Its functions – and the requirements that had to be met in order for it to perform those functions – were misunderstood and neglected. Indeed, well into the 1980s the financial systems of most developing countries were "repressed". The third view on the relationship between finance and development is based on a strong attack against the policy of financial repression and it has led to a strategy of liberalising and strengthening the financial system.

There is a macro–economic branch of the third – or liberalization – view, and a microeconomic branch. The former is associated with the names of Edward Shaw and Ronald McKinnon, and the latter with those of J. D. Von Pischke and Dale Adams and his associates at Ohio State University (OSU). Their common argument is that a financial system which is not constrained by unnecessary regulation will be able to mobilize large volumes of savings; transform them with respect to terms, sizes and risks into investible funds; and allocate these funds to socially valuable investment projects. In this view, financial intermediation is the essence of a financial system. The three main propositions of the advocates of the third view are

(1) that the quantity and quality of financial intermediation that is available in a given society is a very important determinant of development,
(2) that the quantity and quality of financial intermediation is determined nearly exclusively by the economic policy pursued by the respective government and
(3) that the best policy is a policy of drastic deregulation of the financial system.

Focus on the functions of the financial system

The financial system consists of financial institutions, financial markets and financial instruments (or claims). Financial institutions trade financial instruments in financial markets. Those financial institutions which are financial intermediaries buy primary claims from deficit spending units and sell secondary claims to surplus spending units. In other words, they take deposits from savers and lend funds to potential investors. In doing so, they meet a demand on the part of depositors, who want to transfer resources to the future, and a demand on the part of borrowers, who want to use funds before they receive income.

In order to understand why financial intermediation is productive or socially valuable, one has to compare a situation in which financial intermediaries are present with one in which they are non–existent. Without intermediaries, savers would have to hold wealth in the form of real assets or cash, or they would have to incur high transaction costs to find qualified borrowers for direct lending. And if potential investors wished to invest more than the amount of their own savings, they would have to incur high transaction costs to find willing and trusting lenders. Compared with a world of self–financing, intermediation frees savers from the confines of their own personal opportunities to invest in real assets and widens the range of options for investors. Compared with a world of direct lending only, intermediation can reduce the costs of financial transactions considerably. To the extent that saving and investment volumes are dependent on interest rates and the transaction costs of savers and investors, efficient intermediaries will increase saving and investment. In addition, it can be assumed that financial intermediaries are particularly well qualified to select investment projects and to monitor their implementation. Therefore, not only the volume but also the "quality" of investment is increased through intermediation.

An additional, and equally important, function of the financial system is to transform capital through intermediaries or through organized financial markets, whereby liquidity, terms to maturity, lot sizes and the risk characteristics of claims undergo transformation. Financial institutions can issue claims with properties which are more attractive to depositors (savers) (e.g. more liquid or less risky) than those of the claims which the institutions buy from investors or borrowers.

The empirical relationship between growth and savings, which has been mentioned above, is evidence of the macroeconomic benefits of well--developed financial systems: In countries whose financial systems are less restricted and more developed (or "deeper"), a given savings rate will usually be associated with a higher growth rate than one would find in a country with a "repressed" financial system that had the same savings rate. The general finding of numerous econometric studies is that "financial depth", measured as broad money (M_2) over GNP, is about as important for growth as the savings or investment rate.

Financial repression and its consequences

Under the first two views it was believed that the fixing of interest rates at levels below what might be market rates would have important positive effects: It would induce more investment because of lower capital costs, more long–term investment because of the higher interest elasticity of long–term investment, and more social justice because poorer people are assumed to be particularly unable to bear high interest costs. All this seems plausible, but it is basically wrong: either it is inconsistent with empirical evidence or it is based on faulty logic, or both.

First of all, more investment can only be undertaken if more savings are available in a form which is suited for onlending, that is: in the form of financial savings. But low interest rates make people save less or at least save less in the form of financial savings. So financial repression leads to less investable funds and thus to less instead of more investment.

Secondly, even with given savings and investment rates financial repression has a negative effect on the "quality" of investment leading to lower growth. McKinnon (1973) demonstrates this effect as follows: Financial repression normally includes ceilings for interest rates on loans which are below the level that market rates would reach if there were an efficient and properly functioning market for financial services. Because capital is subsidized, borrowing is attractive for some investors with projects which would not yield a high enough return to enable them to pay the market interest rate. Under financial repression, banks will ration credit and grant loans according to non–economic criteria such as political influence. As these criteria of allocation are not designed to exclude borrowers with such unprofitable projects, this allocation system leads to a lower average productivity of all of the investment projects which do receive funding and, in the final analysis, to lower growth rates.

Thirdly, interest ceilings for credit and the credit rationing resulting thereof are also the reason for a negative distributive effect of financial repression. If financial institutions are not allowed to charge "market clearing" rates of interest, bankers will naturally prefer those borrowers whom they regard as personal friends, who have political clout, who can pay bribes, whose credit requests are easy to evaluate, and who request large loans with relatively low administrative costs. Though interest rate ceilings are introduced in order to make credit affordable for lower-income segments of the population this objective of benefitting the poor is never realised. Instead, subsidized credit goes to those who need the subsidies least. There is ample empirical evidence that the "iron law of interest rate restriction" (Gonzalez–Vega, 1984) is valid everywhere.

While financial repression is most likely to have adverse effects on savings, investment, growth and distribution, it has been found to have even more serious negative consequences for financial institutions. Oppressive regulation – and, in particular, government-imposed interest rates which are often below the inflation rate – as well as the granting of far too extensive powers to the central bank, prevent the banking system from fulfilling its economic roles of intermediation and transformation of capital.

First of all, low permissible lending rates force banks to pay only low deposit rates and eliminate the incentives to engage in savings mobilisation efforts. This, in turn reduces the banks' lending capacity in terms of volume and thus prevents them from realising economies of scale and increasing their efficiency. Existing commercial banks therefore only cater to a small, in some cases even a very small, segment of the population and the economy. The majority of the people in the society and their businesses are regularly denied access to banks as far as credit is concerned, and very often they are also not permitted to utilize deposit facilities either. In some countries, e.g. in Africa, the minimum deposit which a client would have to make in order to open an account with one of the private, urban banks exceeds the monthly income of an average wage-earner. In many cases, credit is for all practical purposes reserved for big, export-oriented businesses and for those who have an ownership interest in a bank.

Many governments of developing countries, as well as donor agencies were unhappy with this state of affairs. But instead of creating an environment in which the banks would be in a position to – and have an incentive to – expand and improve both their lending and deposit-taking activities, they chose to make up for the lack of deposits by providing lines of credit – at subsidized rates, and with the request that these funds be distributed by any and all means available.

For commercial banks, the easy access to cheap funds further weakened the incentives to mobilise savings. For the development banks, the funds from the goverment, the central bank or donors were often the only source of loanable funds, and these "banks" were relegated to the position of distributors of externally supplied credit and subsidies. The most important element of credit subsidisation was not the artificially low lending rate, but rather the fact that clever (and influential) borrowers had a good chance of avoiding repayment of their loans altogether. In the final analysis, financial repression leads to a small, inefficient and financially fragile banking system, the unavailability of credit for most potential borrowers, and a conspicuous lack of deposit facilities.

Policy implications: the plea for deregulation

The policy implications of the analysis that has been outlined in the preceding discussion are straightforward. On the macroeconomic level, financial liberalization is advocated by Shaw, McKinnon and their followers. Liberalising interest rates in particular would permit the banking system to perform its true economic function, increase the flow of capital through the financial system, improve allocational efficiency and foster economic growth. In recent years this advice has been followed with considerable success in some parts of the world, notably in East Asia. Important international development institutions like the World Bank have started to make financial liberalization a central element of structural adjustment programmes. This policy reflects the insight that convenient and affordable credit and deposit faciletes are extremely important and valuable for households and small producers. But there are also several cases where financial liberalization has failed because it was undertaken in an unstable macroeconomic environment.

In the context of this study, the microeconomic implications are even more important than the implications for macroeconomic policy. The basic messages are these:

(1) A demand – and not merely a need – for financial services exists within the poorer segments of the population.
(2) People demand credit, and they want to be able to count on having access to fairly priced credit. They do not "need" subsidized loans, and they are able to repay loans if the lender utilizes appropriate monitoring and incentive mechanisms to make them feel obliged to do so.
(3) Even more than credit, poor people in urban and rural areas of developing countries – who save in any case – demand deposit facilities with low transaction costs. A banking system which gives rise to low transaction costs for clients, and pays and charges

reasonably high interest rates can most probably mobilize enough savings to meet the demand of the respective society for investment capital.

(4) Banks which have to struggle to obtain their deposits are highly motivated to lend wisely and to ensure that both their administrative costs and their loan losses remain on an acceptable level.

(5) Banking in the "ambitious" sense of financial intermediation, targeted to a broad segment of the population, is feasible and viable as a commercial undertaking in the developing world. In other words: banking with the poor instead of banking for the poor is called for.

(6) However, this presupposes the existence of a favourable legal and economic environment and of the political resolve not to use the financial system for other purposes.

Banking is seen as an industry that is essentially not different from many others that operate in the economy. It provides services and has certain production costs. If it is left to its own devices and is subject to competitive pressures, the banking industry will supply its products as long as clients are willing and able to pay cost–covering prices for them.

According to this view, development aid projects in support of "finance" should not provide foreign funds, as this would only weaken the savings mobilisation incentives and undermine the local financial system. Instead, it is felt that they should furnish technical assistance to financial institutions and support to government policy–making organizations so that deregulation of the financial sector can be achieved. Technical assistance projects would have to succeed in establishing viable banks and help them learn to be efficient and accessible to a broad clientele. Subsidies should never take the form of subsidized interest rates for borrowers. Subsidies to foster institution–building are legitimate, but they would have to be temporary in nature.

Assessment

We are convinced that this third view is basically correct, i.e. we feel that efficient and effective banking carried on with the general public is possible in developing countries. However, at this point the body of empirical evidence that can be cited in support of this position is limited to individual success stories, and thus one cannot yet say that its validity has been demonstrated conclusively. Moreover, there is clearly a lack of theoretical underpinning for the liberalization view. The proponents of the "OSU approach" have developed their position mainly on the basis of a critique of the prevailing development aid policy. They have put forth a convincing economic philosophy of "free markets for rural finance", but they have not yet provided a formal and explicit model of financial institutions and financial markets. The implicit model being used is one in which financial institutions are monolithic, profit-maximizing firms, and in which financial markets function in essentially the same way as markets for chairs and tables (Stiglitz, 1989). But these two premises are almost certainly wrong, and therefore the plea for deregulation is certainly not enough, i.e. deregulation is not sufficient to solve all of the problems that are characteristic of repressed financial systems. In fact, macroeconomic instability may not be the only reason why free financial markets can fail. The lack of a proper microeconomic foundation does not make the OSU position untenable, but it does make it incomplete.

2.4 The Fourth View: Finance, Institutions, and Incentives

The fourth view about the relationship between finance and development is based on recent advances in the microeconomic theory of organization, finance and markets which have given rise to a broader conceptual framework known as the "new theoretical institutionalism". In the present context the most relevant of its component disciplines is the "economics of information". Joseph Stiglitz contributed greatly to the economics of information and at the same time reshaped our view of financial markets and on the relationship between finance and development[2]. In Stiglitz (1986), he has coined the term "the new development economics" (NDE) or the approach which he and his collaborators pursue.

This fourth view holds that economic development depends more on the availability of "good institutions" than on anything else, and that, in turn, the most important institutional prerequisite is the existence of a good financial sector. Institutions are called good if they provide the type of incentives which promote savings, capital accumulation and allocation in such a way that they lead to growth.

The generic term 'institutions' is used in a broad sense. It includes markets as a special type of institution, with firms and governments also being regarded as basic types of institutions. The financial system is an institution, and its main elements such as specific financial markets and "banks" or financial intermediaries (financial institutions in common terminology) are also institutions.

---

[2] See among other sources his 1986, 1989, 1989a, 1989b, 1991.

In order to appreciate the specific contributions and emphasis of this view it is necessary to start with an understanding of how markets in general and financial markets in particular function or, more specifically, fail to function efficiently. The key to understanding this is to start from the observation that in many markets, notably financial and labour markets, information is asymmetrically distributed and costly, and that it is therefore impossible to write and enforce contracts which would cover all contingencies. Financial contracts almost always create incentive problems which are also characterized as "moral hazard". For this reason, and because of the equally pervasive problem of adverse selection, financial markets do not normally function in the way in which, for instance, Shaw (1973) and McKinnon (1973) and the researchers from the Ohio State University used to think that they functioned[3].

In fact, the economics of information provides reasons to believe that "free financial markets" would not only not function in an optimal way, but rather not function at all (Stiglitz, 1989b). According to this view, one could expect credit rationing and other forms of capital rationing to be pervasive if markets were deregulated completely (Stiglitz/Weiss, 1981): Savers, or banks, would abstain from lending their funds to potential investors because they would be afraid that the information advantage of the potential borrowers would be used against them. However, this is not what happens everywhere and at all times. The reason why we do not observe a general failure of financial markets is that contracts on real–life financial markets include elements which, to a certain extent, "contain" the dangers posed by the basic problems of adverse selection and moral hazard.

A good set of financial institutions, in the broad sense described above, can replace negative incentives by positive incentives at least to some extent and thus enable the financial markets of the real world to come closer to the utopian state of "perfect financial markets" than merely "free" markets could ever be. As Stiglitz rightly points out (e.g. in Stiglitz, 1989, 1989a), the lack of good financial systems is one of the main reasons for the dismal economic situation of most countries in the developing world and the former Eastern bloc. It is the task of financial inter-mediaries to accumulate and to allocate capital and to monitor its use. The banking system is not a passive or neutral conduit for capital, it is rather the central allocation, monitoring and accounting system of society.

---

[3] But see also McKinnon (1986) and (1989) where earlier views are revised in the light of the work of Stiglitz/Weiss (1981), and most recently McKinnon (1991).

It might be easier to understand the practical implications of the fourth view of finance and development if we contrast it with the first three views.

The difference with regard to the first view is clearly the importance that is attached to the process of allocation and monitoring. The third view ("liberalization view") rightly stresses the importance of financial markets. In this respect it is similar to the fourth view. But the third view holds that a financial system which is not "repressed" would by itself function optimally. In view of the pervasiveness and importance of information and incentive problems on financial markets, such optimism is unfounded. Indeed, "by suggesting that markets by themselves would take care of matters, these theories (of the merits of liberalization) have done a disservice" (Stiglitz, 1989b, p. 20).

This argument indicates that there is a certain similarity between the fourth and the second view. But the proponents of the second view implicitly – and even explicitly – believe that governments and other administrative bodies would be able to avoid the mistakes which occur when markets do not function optimally ("market failures") by allocating capital according to non-market standards and that they would thus improve allocation. However, no convincing arguments have been presented to show why government and other bureaucrats would do a better job of solving the information and incentive problems than the market has historically done.

The fourth view takes an intermediate position between the second and third views: Financial markets are important, and may be helpful "institutions", but they are not likely to function perfectly. And basically the same thing can be said of governmental and other administrative bodies. Therefore the alternative "either markets or bureaucracies" is ill-conceived. This is not the issue! Instead the issue is which institution functions in what way, on the basis of the information it has and the incentives to which its agents are subject.

Institutions can themselves be regarded as the product of long-term competitive or market processes. The "market" to which we are referring here serves as a selection mechanism: There may be something like competition between different institutional forms trying to survive in a contest to solve a real world problem. But due to the same information and incentive problems with which any financial institution must contend, namely adverse selection and moral hazard, the set of institutions evolving from this process of "natural selection" is not likely to be optimal. And the market allocation brought about by a given set of institutions is also not likely to be "optimal". In technical terms, a market equilibrium is almost always not constrained Pareto-efficient (Greenwald/Stiglitz, 1988). This has a very important implication: In contrast to the liberalization and deregulation philosophy underlying the third view, there is always room for interventions which can bring about improvements in the allocation of resources. Put simply, development aid measures directed at the financial system can be welfare–enhancing. Of course, there is no guarantee that they will be.

If one wanted to improve the performance of the financial sector of a developing country, and, more specifically, make its financial institutions more efficient, one would have to study in great detail how the existing institutions go about solving the information and incentive problems they face – or at least mitigating their effects. Stiglitz and his various collaborators have done this at a great length. They have studied extensively the functioning of financial markets and (narrowly defined) financial institutions and the efficiency properties of financial arrangements in a world in which information is unevenly distributed and where, consequently, incentives have to be provided through contract design. More important than the specific findings of these researchers (see e.g. Bardhan, 1989, and Braverman/Guasch, 1986 and 1989) are, in our view, their methodology and the implications of their style of analysis.

To summarize the main elements of the fourth view:

(1) Finance in the sense of financial system is extremely important for development.
(2) The operations of financial markets are subject to constraints posed by the pervasive problems of information and incentives.
(3) Financial markets do function, but they are not likely to function as well as they would in a world where information was available at no cost and evenly distributed.
(4) Market allocations are not always efficient in reality, and institutions are not always optimally designed.
(5) It is possible to find ways of influencing market allocations and the set and structure of existing institutions in such a way that the economic welfare of people (target groups) can be increased.
(6) However, it is difficult to find the right form and the right starting point for intervention.
(7) Intervention should aim at improving the way institutions function, it should try to improve the relevant system of incentives.
(8) In order to avoid counterproductive intervention it is imperative to begin by analysing the status quo, i.e. how the relevant market and institutions function in their current state.

3. Synopsis and Evaluation

Table 2 on the next page gives a synopsis of the four views. As can easily be seen, they differ very much in terms of how they define "finance", how much confidence they have in the functional strenghts of financial markets, the standards for assessing a financial system and, finally, what they consider to be the optimal development aid strategy.

Each of the first three views contains more than just a grain of truth: indeed, they all provide valuable insights and help illuminate important parts of the overall picture. Thus, while developing countries do not always need a transfer of real capital – and therefore an injection of financial capital – under certain conditions they do. The present situation of several countries in Latin America seems to require such an external push (Dornbusch, 1990). Target groups among the poor have always been hard to reach via development aid measures. It is always worth trying to do something in order to improve their access to quality financial services. Deregulation is probably the most promising agenda for improving the performance of a financial system. In particular the regulation of interest rates should be abolished in most countries where this has not yet been done. But one should not expect too much from deregulation.

Although the fourth view is the least operational of the four in terms of how its implications translate into specific policy initiatives, we think that it has the greatest significance of any of them for analysis as well as policy. It provides a deeper understanding of the problems of financial systems, and this type of understanding must be acquired before action plans can be drawn up. As the following chapters should demonstrate, the present study is strongly influenced by, and in fact adopts, the fourth view.

View	Time	What is relevant about "finance"?	Central assumption why finance matters	Finance has an impact on ...	Policy implications and recommendations	Standards for evaluating financial systems	Empirical evidence for success of policy
1.	50s/60s	capital accumulation	macro-economic production function	GNP-growth	transfer capital (and technology)	capital stock; savings and investment rates	yes, but mixed
2.	60s - 80s	capital accumulation and allocation to target groups	very imperfect goods and capital markets	sectoral growth, income and production	design "targeted" and subsidized credit programmes	outreach of credit supply to many segments of society ("optimal access")	partially yes, but with negative side effects on fin. institutions and markets
3.	70s/80s	mobilization, transformation and allocation of capital	perfect markets and efficient institutions (only) if liberalized	a. quantity and quality capital b. supply and cost of financial services	set up viable non-subsidizing financial institutions in a liberalized and stable environment	low-cost/complex array of financial services from efficient and stable institutions	yes, but only in a stable economy yes, but not enough
4.	80s/90s	as above plus coordination of expectations and incentives	pervasive information and incentive problems	the functioning of markets and institutions	analyze and rationalize the incentive structure	as above plus efficient incentive structures within institutions and vis-à-vis clients	multiple financial institutions exist and are viable

Table 2: *The importance of "finance" for development: Four views on what "finance" is, why it is assumed to be important, and how it should be supported*

C

ON THE DUALISTIC STRUCTURE OF
THE FINANCIAL SYSTEM

1. Introduction

It is common among development economists to distinguish between a formal and an informal economic sector. The latter is believed to be a segment of the economy and of the society at large which encompasses the poorer strata of the population and, therefore, also the main target groups of development strategies geared to alleviating poverty and promoting self-reliant development.

This chapter attempts to clarify the meaning of the dichotomy "formal--informal" in light of the aforementioned new theoretical institutionalism (the fourth view). Special attention is given to contract enforcement, which is a prerequisite for allowing members of a society to enter into binding arrangements with each other. We will explain how the availability of outside enforcement mechanisms, or the lack thereof, might influence the behaviour of economic agents and shape the functioning and the form of economic institutions.

Until quite recently, the informal financial sector did not play any significant role in official development programmes. An internal World Bank report mentions 1978 as the year of change (World Bank, 1983). Prior to 1978 there was little systematic effort to investigate the structure of formal financial markets, and informal financial markets received next to no attention. Policy recommendations were largely based on the diagnosis of a general capital shortage. The traditional Development Finance Institutions are an outgrowth of this orientation. A more recent

30

important for the effectiveness of development policy but, unfortunately, it is believed to be "out of sight" (World Bank, 1989a, p. 6).

It was not until the 1970s that actors in the informal sector became the subject of systematic research. The well-known Kenya studies conducted by the ILO in 1972 represented an important breakthrough concentrating on the "real" sector (Hart, 1973). As a consequence, by the early 1980s, most development banks were charged with the task of pursuing more grassroots–oriented development objectives focussing on the informal non–financial sector, especially small entrepreneurs. This new orientation implicitly confronted the traditional DFIs with what appeared to be a fundamental dilemma of economic viability versus target--group–oriented behaviour.

Additional research concentrated on the informal financial sector. The investigations that were conducted during this period called attention to the special quality of its financial institutions and arrangements, stressing among other things, the flexibilty of these arrangements and their low transaction costs.[4] Despite these research efforts, the informal financial sector and its institutions are not areas of primary emphasis for financial development policy today (World Bank, 1989a).

Section 2 of this chapter outlines the prevailing, descriptive view of the informal financial sector as well as the key concepts and structures which have been identified on the basis of empirical research. A comprehensive description of the unique characteristics of financial institutions in the informal sector is not provided, as it can be found in a study recently published by the OECD (see Germidis *et al.*, 1991).

Sections 3 and 4 concentrate on the specific organizational patterns that characterize (and distinguish) financial transactions in the formal and informal sectors. We will concentrate on the legal infrastructure (LI) of a country, which in most developing countries covers only part of the economy. We will argue that the degree to which the economic agents in a given country have access to its legal infrastructure (especially with respect to the judicial enforcement of private agreements) allows a relevant distinction to be made between formal and informal economic activity. Furthermore, the limited accessability of the LI may be one of the underlying reasons for the emergence of informal financial relationships (and institutions). In the next chapter, this insight will prove helpful in analysing individual types of financial institutions. Section 5 of the present chapter cites and discusses briefly two explanations for the existence and functioning of the informal financial sector. One of them emphasizes the

---

[4]   See, for instance, Seibel/Koll, 1968; Gonzalez-Vega, 1986; Stiglitz, 1986; Chandarvakar, 1989; Adams, 1992; Seibel/Marx, 1987

functioning of the informal financial sector. One of them emphasizes the influence of "repressive" financial market regulation on the development of the respective financial sectors, whereas the second one sees financial dualism as an outgrowth of the general dualistic structure of the economic system in developing countries. The concluding section (6) outlines some lessons for development policy.

2. Informal Sector Activities

The economic structure of developing countries today is normally described as being dualistic, distinguishing between a formal and an informal sector. Usually the formal sector is seen as encompassing all economic activities which fall under the relevant rules and regulations in a given country. Economic activities which are not covered by these rules and regulations are called informal. According to the literature, the informal sector makes a significant – and in some cases, sizeable – contribution to the production of goods and services in many developing countries; the share contributed by the informal sector tends to be inversely related to the country's level of development. In the case of Peru, for example, the informal sector contributes an estimated 38% of GDP, 70% of construction activity and even as much as 85% of public transportation activity (de Soto, 1989). The World Bank estimates that the informal sector accounts for between 30% and 70% of total employment in developing countries (World Bank, 1989a).

Like the real economy, the financial system of developing countries also contains formal and informal segments, or sectors. Institutions and transactions which are directly subject to national financial market regulation (banking legislation and supervision) are normally considered to be part of the formal sector. These institutions include public and private commercial banks, specialized financial institutions (including regional banks, development banks and long-term venture financiers), mutual and municipal/communal savings and loan associations, as well as some non-bank financial institutions such as insurance companies, postal savings banks, deposit insurance corporations and, in some countries, regulated markets for equity and bonds. Formalized ("registered") financial corporations which are, however, not subject to banking supervision – such as credit cooperatives, leasing and hire-purchase companies and most NGOs engaged in financial activities as well as other non-bank financial institutions (provident funds and pension schemes) – are often classified as semi-formal institutions. But for the present discussion they are adequately listed as formal in the sense of having recourse to the legal infrastructure.

Informal financial institutions, on the other hand, fall completely outside the legal infrastructure of the economy and constitute the informal financial sector. They are not registered; they are not subject to supervision by the banking and monetary authorities; often they do not comply with common bookkeeping standards; and, not surprisingly, they are not reflected in the official statistics on the depth and breadth of the national financial market. Informal financial institutions include money lenders (including independent bankers, landlords, traders, family members and friends), mutual savings and credit associations (rotating savings and credit associations: RoSCAs, tontines) and other self-help organizations.[5]

Proceeding from this classification of the financial system along institutional lines, and on the basis of empirical studies that have been conducted in developing countries in Latin America, Africa and Asia, it is possible to identify and define forms of activities as being typical of the formal and informal sectors, respectively (Germidis *et al.*, 1991). In particular, formal–sector institutions may be characterized by a concentration of business activity in urban areas. In terms of attracting funds, formal–sector institutions rely to a large extent on government-distributed or foreign capital; savings and deposits are of secondary importance, in some cases they are even forbidden. Similarly lending activities focus on large individual amounts and are thus regularly allocated to large, established, private and government–owned enterprises in the modern and industrial sector. Processing of transactions entails a great deal of red tape and must conform to fixed bureaucratic procedures. The resulting high transaction costs for banks and customers reinforce the bias towards relatively large loans.

By contrast, the business of informal–sector financial institutions concentrates on loans and deposits for small firms and households which usually belong to the informal sector. Often, loans are granted without formal collateral. In these cases, familiarity with the personal cirumstances of the debtor serve as a substitute for collateral. Social sanctions such as those that may exist, for example, between members of a family or a village or a religious community, also serve as substitutes for the possibility of recourse to legal enforcement. Furthermore, credit terms are typically adopted to the situation of the client. The total amount lent, as well as the number and the frequency of installments, is fitted to the expected cashflow of the debtor. For him or her there is little, if any, paperwork involved in applying for a loan.

---

5   For a more comprehensive list see Chapter A, p. 7

To sum up, flexibility of loan terms and adaption of loan management to the personal situation of the client are generally judged to be the most salient operational characteristics of informal financial institutions. It should be kept in mind that these financial activities are not monitored by banking supervisory authorities and that they are, in fact, tax-exempt.

3. Financial Dualism and the Legal Infrastructure

What is special about informality? Rather than collecting bits and pieces of evidence that give an impression of informal transactions and informal institutions, we will start with a somewhat general hypothesis concerning the constraints that determine modes of transacting in the economic system in general, and in the financial system in particular.

Our hypothesis is this: The mode of transacting – i.e. a contract in the case of a unique transaction, and an institution in the case of a number of repeated transactions – is shaped by the type of enforcement mechanism that is available. There may be different types of enforcement mechanisms: social sanctions between members of a community, or a family, for instance; or an illegal, possibly violent form of prosecution by a gang; or legal prosecution through official agents like policemen or sheriffs.

To give an example, loan arrangement can be supported by formal collateral if in case of non-fulfillment of contract terms the lender has the right, and indeed the practical opportunity, to liquidate the pledged asset. Here, the right and its enforceability are crucial. The same collateral will be of little use if the creditor is unable to execute his claim.

A lack of enforceability using legal means, however, is characteristic of informal transactions. Social sanctions and norms, or moral or family ties might then substitute for legal enforcement. In some cases, social norms impose even stricter constraints on the behaviour of economic agents than would legal sanctions. A well-known example is the arrangement which amounts to the enslavement of a non-complying debtor ("bondage"), which is found even now in remote areas of India.

Apart from social and ethical norms, the absence of legally enforceable contractual stipulations induces economic agents to develop an intelligent contractual form that diminishes the risk of breach of contract by anyone party to the arrangement.

Using the possibility of recourse to the legal enforcement mechanism as a distinguishing characteristic, a more precise definition of formal and informal economic activities can now be developed: A transaction between economic agents is called formal if for enforcement purposes it relies on the legal system of society. Otherwise it is called informal. This definition is equally valid for both financial transactions and financial institutions. Besides not being registered, informal financial institutions largely rely on informal transactions.

A schematic presentation of the relationship between the legal, the economic and the financial system is provided in Figure 2. The two heavily outlined segments delineate the two sectors of society whose interaction generates formal economic activity, namely, the economic system and the legal system. The latter not only comprises all laws and regulations, but also all actors and activities which are involved in the supervision and enforcement of the codified rules. The economic system contains all actors and activities which deal with exchange and production. Where the two systems overlap, i.e. when economic activities take place under the rule of laws etc., one speaks of formal economic activity. It is fully subject to the conditions of the legal infrastructure or legal system.

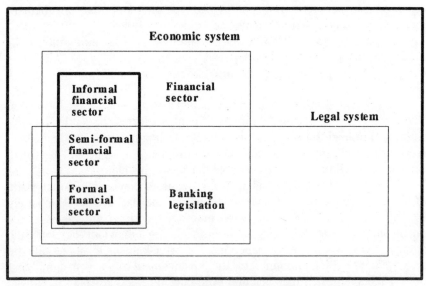

Figure 2: The formal, semiformal, and informal financial sectors and their relation to the economic and legal systems

Outside of the overlapping area in Figure 2 above there is, on the one hand, the non-economic legal infrastructure (constitutional and criminal law, for example) and, on the other, the economic activities which are beyond the reach of the legal infrastructure and which are referred to as the informal sector.

A similar division into formal and informal sectors applies in all sub-systems of economic life, and, thus, in the financial system as well. The situation is more complicated inasmuch as there is a segment of the legal system which is specifically related to financial institutions and transactions (banking laws in addition to governmental supervision and enforcement). It is a proper subset of both the legal system and the economic system, giving rise to the tripartite division shown in Figure 2. The term formal financial sector is then employed to refer to that part of the financial market which is subject to the relevant banking supervision. Of course, institutions in the formal financial sector are also subject to all other constraints which constitute the relevant legal system. Financial institutions and transactions which have recourse to this system in general, but are not subject to banking supervision are referred to as semi-formal. Institutions or actors who refrain from taking recourse to the legal infrastructure are, appropriately, referred to as informal.

As mentioned above, legal infrastructure is the generic term for all structural and procedural aspects of contracting and "public" enforcement. It comprises laws and regulations governing contracts, corporations, market entry and exit, competition and anti-trust regulation, and most important, claim settlement. Interpretation and application of these laws and regulations are effectuated by a network of courts, lawyers, prosecutors, enforcement agents (police, prison, bailiff/sheriff).

It is helpful to regard the legal infrastructure as a productive segment of society. By making use of physical resources, such as court buildings, and human resources – prosecutors, lawyers, judges and so forth – and by relying on a set of more or less general rules, the expectation is established that contract enforcement will be available on demand. The role of the legal infrastructure in terms of its input into almost all aspects of economic production and welfare is pervasive. In industrialized countries the legal infrastructure is permanently available and almost free of charge. Nevertheless, the incidence of court cases is relatively small compared to the number of times that contractual relations are established, be it explicitly or implicitly, with other members of society. The legal infrastructure therefore provides an enforcement mechanism whose efficiency is inversely related to the actual demand for claim settlement. Its primary function consists in deterring economic agents from breach of contract.

Evidently, it is rather expensive to supply a legal infrastructure (i.e. to provide for its establishment and maintenance), which also requires a great deal of financial and human capital. Since its establishment costs are high, the provision of legal infrastructure in most developing countries is restricted to specific economic activities or agents, i.e. those within the formal sector. Many people cannot reasonably expect that the legal infrastructure would help them enforce contracts, and they are thus prevented from entering into such contracts in the first place. This supports the view that the economic structure is correctly described as dualistic rather than as a continuum of sectors ranging from completely formal economic activities to completely informal activities.

The "entry barriers" to using the legal infrastructure may be quite high. Hernando de Soto estimated the height of these barriers in the case of the registration of a small workshop, consisting of two sewing machines, located outside Lima, Peru; he concluded that one lawyer and his four assistants would need a total of 289 eight-hour days to get the workshop formally established if they were to comply strictly with the prevailing formal rules and regulations. In New York, the same registration would require only half a day (de Soto, 1989).

To sum up, we suggest a notion of informality that is characterized by the lack of something, namely the lack of access to the legal infrastructure of the country. This characterization of informality casts doubt on the value of some recent attempts to describe institutions in the informal sector rather euphemistically as "ingenious" or "fascinating".

4. Characteristics of Informal Financial Sector Activity

Figure 2 above is intended as an aid in ordering and clarifying the multitude of terms that are currently being applied to formal and informal financial institutions. Note that in many cases the assignment of an activity to the formal or informal sector may be a matter of choice, i.e. something which can be decided by the contracting parties. This is particularly evident in the case of illegal business transactions, such as the production and sale of drugs, an area which often plays an economically significant role in Latin America and Southeast Asia.

Even in the case of small savings and credit transactions, however, there is a genuine choice available in many developing countries between joining an informal rotating savings and credit association (RoSCA) or a (semi-formal) credit cooperative. This, in turn, gives rise to the question of the economically relevant implications if recourse to the legal system is more or less voluntarily is forgone. Without the legal system, the arrangements that are made between two parties have to be self-enforcing, since no recourse will be taken to outside enforcement. This means that a form of arrangement has to be made in which fulfillment of the contract in accordance with the agreed terms appears reasonable and plausible to all parties not only at the beginning of the relationship of cooperation, but also throughout its duration. Having to rely on self-enforcement will result in a considerable reduction in the number and types of possible cooperation and exchanges between economic agents, and thus in a loss of gains from cooperation and exchange.

The lack of recourse to the legal system affects the nature of financial relationships in particular because by their very nature they involve longer-term, intertemporal relationships between two or more contracting parties. The span of time which lies between performance and counter-performance in the case of a credit makes it necessary to have an explicit or implicit form of bonding on the borrower's part. If there were no bond, the lender (or depositor) would have to fear that the borrower might simply refuse to repay when the loan is due, and therefore he would not lend or deposit his money in the first place. If there is not recourse to the legal infrastructure, bonding is affected in two ways. On the one hand, the available means of providing creditor protection through ownership-transfer are extremely limited. The creditor has only very few ways of limiting the risk of default. This is further exacerbated by the informality of the borrower, who, for that very reason, is not required to prepare a balance sheet and/or is not bound to comply with the relevant bookkeeping rules. On the other hand, there is also no rule of limited liability for the protection of debtors in the informal sector. Honour, social standing or even the life of a person may substitute for wealth or collateral. It is interesting to note that in some cases the informal ties are so strong that a legal measure prohibiting the inheritance of unwritten debt by the heirs (who have to work off the debt in the form of bonded labour) has actually been ignored – as reported in India in the 1970s (Wolf, 1984).

The failure to take recourse to the legal system thus heightens the contractual risks for both parties while increasing the number of ways in which a contract can be set up (for example, through unlimited liability). The relatively high risk of exploitation on both sides also explains why arrangements in the informal sector are preferably made with family businesses.

Another example of self-enforcing arrangements may be found in many group-related financial arrangements. They take advantage of so-called peer-monitoring. The term "peer-monitoring" describes the social controls within a group and it is positively correlated to the homogeneity of the group in terms of kinship, sex, ethnic membership and the proximity of the members to each other. The latter in particular makes it possible for information to be distributed symmetrically among group members. Peer-monitoring is often made effective by introducing an element of reciprocity, for instance in rotating savings and credit funds (see Chapter D below).

Self–enforcing arrangements, therefore, are frequently found – and are frequently successful – outside the formal financial sector. Group credit schemes and rotating savings and credit associations serve as two prominent examples. The former relies heavily on social control among its members, which is rendered effective by joint liability combined with credit disbursement being conditional upon satisfactory repayment by other group members. Indigenous informal financial institutions, such as RoSCAs, are built around the principle of reciprocity. Further examples of self–monitoring or self–enforcing arrangements in the informal financial sector include the merging of several economically distinct and separate transactions into one overall arrangement. These so–called interlinked transactions play a special role in financing, share–cropping and marketing in the agricultural sector (Braverman/Stiglitz, 1982).

5. Interrelationships of Formal and Informal Financial Markets

Although formal and informal economic arrangements can be distinguished, there may well be an intensive relationship between them. This may take the form of competition, complementarity, or cooperation (cf. Germidis *et al.*, 1991, Chapter 2). If rigid regulation of the formal financial sector causes financial transactions to be shifted to the less or non–regulated semi–formal or informal sectors, competition develops. Financial market policy, which has typically been repressive and interventionist in developing countries, entails strictly regulated interest rates for savings and credit, frequently without regard to actual inflation rates, rigid control of foreign exchange markets as well as the weakening or, in many cases, the outright elimination of competition on the savings and credit market. These and other aspects may enhance the growth prospects of the tax– and regulation–free "informals". For this reason some economists believe that liberalization of the financial market in the sense of reducing the degree of regulation would more or less put the informal financial sector "out of business."

Other authors observe a complementary relation between the formal and informal sectors. They stress the connection between economic activity in the informal real sector, on the one hand, and the informal financial sector, on the other. According to this view, the development of informal financial relationships is an outgrowth of the dual overall social structure in these countries: Informal financial institutions are regarded as being the logical, "rightful" providers of financial services to informal–sector businesses.

Figure 2 above shows that the two positions are not necessarily contradictory. Repressive regulation of the financial market relates above all to the boundary line between the formal and semi-formal sectors. The emphasis on the dual social structures, on the other hand, applies primarily to the boundary line between semi-formal and informal sectors. Moreover, both views point to the importance of the legal infrastructure as a criterion for assigning financial relationships to the formal or the informal sector.

The third type of relationship is cooperation. Consider, for example, the case of a farmer who markets cash crops on the (formal) market and at the same time invests the proceeds in his local moneylending business. In this case, informal credit activity is being refinanced with funds from (formal-sector) economic activity. If the farmer receives a loan from a commercial bank, a credit chain extending from the urban formal financial institution to the rural informal economy is established in which the moneylender is operating as a financial intermediary. Other, less sophisticated examples of intersectoral finance include the rotating savings association that deposits its money in a commercial bank, or traders selling in the formal goods market while extending informal credit to their family business suppliers (Krahnen/Nitsch, 1987).

Given the relatively high incidence and volume of intersectoral finance, the question is whether it should not become a leading issue in development finance. One important intersectoral concept will be discussed briefly. The strategy of linking formal financial institutions to informal self-help groups (SHG) has recently gained prominence (Seibel, 1989). The idea is to preserve the strengths of existing informal financial institutions, namely their appropriate organizational principles and their flexibility, while at the same time enhancing their financial impact through formal-sector assistance, both financial and technical.

A direct relationship between a bank and an existing self-help group is referred to as linking. If, on the other hand, the relevant SHGs are established simply because of the credit facility, the credit transaction is called "group lending." Recent experiences reported by a pilot project in Indonesia seem to be rather positive, with a substantial disbursement volume and an exceptionally good repayment record (Seibel, 1991).

A conclusive evaluation of these and other experiences is not yet possible, however. Eventually it will be necessary to assess:

1. how SHGs have been able to retain their self-enforcing internal structure and cohesion, while at the same time distributing additional, externally supplied funds were to be distributed among group members;

2. how SHGs and, even more importantly, their individual members, managed to cross the border between informal and formal activity;
3. how the permanence of the supply of financial services (lending and deposits) to the group members was ensured and communicated to them.

A second linking technique involves the activities of an NGO which serves as a financial intermediary between an SHG and a formal financial bank. Again, initial experiences in the Indonesian experiment are encouraging (Seibel, 1991).

The strength of an NGO intermediary, namely its social-welfare orientation, its professional involvement with target-group-oriented policymaking and its function as a donor-sponsored provider of technical assistance to small-scale economic activity is, from another angle, probably the major weakness of this type of indirect linking project. For one thing, NGOs are almost never truly self-reliant. Consequently, their operations are bound to be relatively short-lived: after all, they have to ensure that they will continue to receive regular support from their financiers, who, in turn, press for innovative approaches rather than assigning priority to stable and continuous day-to-day work. Secondly, since the contact between bank and customer is more distant than in the case of direct linking, the participating banks and SHGs (or their members) would prefer to interact directly with each other and will use the NGO as a middleman only if it is advantageous for them to do so. Thus, the viability of NGOs in this role will hinge on their ability to provide subsidies, be it in the form of technical assistance, credit guarantee schemes, or similar devices.

6. Lessons for Development Policy

The material presented in this chapter has made it clear that the informal financial sector can under no circumstances be regarded as a no-man's land of financial institutions. On the contrary: it is full of numerous types of institutions which, in contrast to the formal sector, owe their existence and continued viability to self-stabilizing arrangements. Recognizing these structures and utilizing them to the greatest extent possible to promote development is one of the main concerns of development finance today. The services offered by formal and informal financial institutions differ in terms of their production technology rather than the type of service provided. Therefore, they may substitute or complement each other, depending on the specific circumstances.

With respect to institution building, the relatively small range of experience that has been gained to date, permits two tentative conclusions to be drawn:

1. Financial institutions in the informal sector are viable due to the fact that conditions conducive to the functioning of informal values such as reciprocity are used to good advantage. Formal and semi-formal financial institutions which want to become involved in the informal sector can therefore learn a great deal about the special parameters that operate in this sector by examining the existing institutions in terms of their purpose and their stability.
2. Financial institutions in the informal sector are fragile, precisely because they are based on relational principles, such as reciprocity, or tribal bonds. Thus, for example, artificially expanding a previously viable rotating savings and credit association by increasing its membership can lead to internal collapse. By the same token, linking a bank and an SHG may erode the original feeling of solidarity within the group in favour of fragmented, differentiated interests on the part of the membership, thus jeopardizing the NGO's cohesion over the longer term.

The extent to which informal, semiformal or formal financial institutions may be used to implement specific development policies such as target-group-oriented credit schemes, depends crucially upon the internal consistency of the financial institution under consideration, and the scope and scale of financial activities envisaged. A general prescription is unlikely to emerge. Rather, an analysis of the capabilities, efficiency, and stability of every single financial institution is required. Chapter D will outline some general criteria for the evaluation of financial institutions, and will present a series of examples.

D

INSTITUTIONAL ANALYSIS

1. Problem and Methodology

In this chapter, theoretical institutionalism (the "fourth view" mentioned above) is applied to the analysis of several types of financial institutions. The central issue in all of these cases relates to the incentives and opportunities available to the members of specific institutions and their clients. Important questions are: How are the scope and the quality of financial services offered by a specific institution related to its governance structure? Is there an incentive for the institutions' management to operate in a cost-effective and efficient way? Does the existing institutional (internal) stability allow for significant quantitative growth? With respect to its clientele, to what extent is the institution "bound" to a specified target group? We have selected a number of financial institutions and instruments according to their prominence, as we perceive it, in today's debate about the new development economics (see World Bank, 1989).

In section 2 of this chapter we will analyse in detail one class of institutions, namely those in which the aspect of groups plays a dominant role, notably Rotating Saving and Credit Associations, Credit Cooperatives, and Group Lending. Our main reason for concentrating on them is threefold. First, we think that they are particularly relevant for the target groups to which we refer in this study, namely the poorer segments of the population. Second, we focus on group-related institutions because we feel that in the analytical literature on development finance they have up to now been largely overlooked. Third, we have gained the impression from discussions on a more practical level that there are many serious misunderstandings relating to these institutions and their potential in assisting economic development.

Section 3 discusses other financial institutions, notably Revolving Credit Funds and Credit Guarantee Schemes. That section also covers institutions that are of special interest for the development of a financial infrastructure due to their sizeable branch networks, namely the Postal Savings Banks and other large banks. Since our presentation is intended to be methodological in nature, we will not deal with every institution at equal length. Instead, emphasis is placed on the generation of interesting hypotheses concerning the interplay of the incentives of individual agents, the constraints imposed on them by a specific institutional form, and the economic or financial function which this form fulfills. The chapter will close with an attempt to summarize the basic relationship between institutional structure and institutional performance, both in terms of efficiency and in terms of target group orientation. This comparative institutional analysis is designed to serve as a basis for deducing general policy options regarding institution–building which will be developed in the remaining chapters.

In the following discussion we use the terms governance structure or (corporate) constitution interchangeably; they designate the system of incentives and of rights (and opportunities) of individuals to decide and to act in the framework of any given institution. It is our hypothesis that the governance structure of a financial institution is of crucial importance for the type and quality of the services it offers, and ultimately for its ability to survive over time and to provide its services on a lasting basis.

2. Group–oriented Financial Institutions and Programmes

2.1 General Orientation

Financial contracts such as loans cover a certain time span. The loan is paid out "now", repayment is expected "later". This difference between payment and repayment times creates a problem in contracting because the "motives" of the borrower change as time passes: Before he or she obtains a loan, the borrower wants to pay back at the agreed time because otherwise it would not be possible to obtain the loan. But once the loan is received by the borrower, his or her preference changes, and he or she would "rather not repay". This is quite natural, and it is forseeable. If the lender is not stupid he anticipates this change of preferences, and the loan contract will not be concluded in the first place. Thus, both sides will initially be strongly interested in finding ways to prevent a subsequent shifting of preferences.

As Chapter C has explained, the legal infrastructure is a device which helps borrower and lenders because it substitutes the initial genuine, but temporary preference to repay by the lasting desire to avoid trouble. This is an easy solution to the incentive problem of financial contracting. But in some cases this solution, i.e. relying on the legal infrastructure, is not feasible. Therefore, those financial transactions or contracts which we call informal must, by definition, find other solutions. That is why they have to rely on a particularly skillful and even imaginative design of the contractual relationship between the parties. Combining transactions of a different nature, establishing long-term relationships and (thus) creating some form of mutual contractual and non-contractual obligations are techniques which provide incentives for fulfilling contractual obligations without threatening to use the legal infrastructure. Technically speaking, interlinked transactions and reciprocity arrangements can make contracts, in particular financial and other time-spanning contracts, self-enforcing.

Financial relationships in the so-called informal financial sector have no choice but to use arrangements which substitute inside or self-enforcement for outside enforcement or (the threat of) recourse to the legal infrastructure. However, since the use of the legal infrastructure may be expensive and difficult to secure, and since the threat to use it thus may not always solve all problems of financial contracting, financial institutions in the formal and semi-formal financial sectors may also be well-advised to use self-enforcing mechanisms in their financial arrangements. That is why group-related financial institutions appear to be so promising in development finance, and why they deserve a closer look.

The use of groups in lending to the broad masses of the poorer population in developing countries has obvious benefits in so far as it can rely on peer pressure. In addition it may benefit from peer-monitoring and economize on information costs when the selection of group members is done by the group itself. Group-related institutions and methods in the formal and semi-formal financial sector would seem to copy the strengths of the informal financial sectors. In order to ascertain whether this generally held belief is justified, this section looks in detail at three institutions or arrangements which share the attribute of being group related. They are the rotating savings and credit associations which are now generally known under their acronym RoSCA (Von Pischke, 1992), credit (and savings) cooperatives, and group-lending schemes set up by banks and, more often, by NGOs.

According to the general methodological orientation described in the introduction to this chapter, we will ask the following four questions:

1. How do they operate?

2. What services do they provide?
3. Assuming they are viable, why do they survive ?
4. What are their limitations and what are the risks they face?

for each of the three types of group–related institutions and programmes. The answers to the first two questions constitute what we call the "analytical description", those to the last two questions result in an "evaluation". After the institutions have been analysed in this way one by one, section 2.5 will attempt to put the pieces together in a comparative institutional assessment.

2.2 Rotating Savings and Credit Associations (RoSCAs)

2.2.1 Analytical Description

How does a rotating credit and savings association (RoSCA) operate? A RoSCA is a group of limited size whose members meet at regular intervals to contribute a predetermined savings "deposit" to the group fund, with all such deposits being of equal size. The sum total of the savings collected at a given meeting is given to a single member. At the next meeting, the procedure is repeated, with a different member receiving all of the money collected. One after another, each of the members is eligible to receive the contributions of all of the other members, and when all of the members have had their turn, the cycle is complete and a new round may start. Often, in the following round the sequence in which the members receive the money is reversed.

There may be an organizer, quite often a woman, who is herself a member of the RoSCA. Her duty is to collect the (uniform) savings "deposits" from each member and to pass the sum total over to the designated recipient. There are a variety of different arrangements in terms of the sequence of allocations to members. In a "standard" RoSCA this sequence is fixed in advance. Each member knows from the outset when it will be her turn to receive the money in the fund. The sequence of allocations may also be determined by chance. In this case, those members of the group who have not yet been recipients in the ongoing cycle participate in what amounts to a lottery. Thus, the probability of becoming the recipient increases as the cycle progresses. A third arrangement which is also quite common is to establish an auction mechanism. At every meeting the sum total is given to the member who is willing to accept the greatest discount from the standard amount, thereby reducing the contribution required from each of the other members or leaving a part of the collected money for a common purpose such as setting up a group fund for emergencies or for lending to group members. Obviously, a member who is in urgent need of cash can bid the discount up to the point where he or she is designated as the recipient. By determining the amount which each member must pay into the fund and ends up in receiving, the auction mechanism indirectly determines the level of the "interest payments" which a recipient with urgent needs must make and which the more patient members receive. While a cycle is in progress, only those members who have not yet been recipients of the fund are eligible to participate in the auction.

It should be mentioned for the sake of completeness that there are also rotating and non–rotating pure savings groups, in which funds may or may not be deposited with a commercial bank. Finally, savings and credit associations may also be non–rotating (see Kropp *et al.*, 1989). In the following discussion we will focus exclusively on the standard RoSCA form (World Bank, 1989a, p. 114).

What are the financial services that RoSCAs can provide? There are basically four services that RoSCAS can offer to their members: the accumulation of savings, the transformation of the size of savings, intermediation between depositors and creditors and, in some cases, insurance against individual hazards.

The first function or service of a RoSCA is that it makes the members save regularly and thus accumulate savings. Whether or not the accumulation of savings will have lasting effects for the individual member and for the group as a whole depends on how the money is used once it is the individual member's turn to receive the contributions of the entire group.

The mutual agreement between the members obviously has the effect of educating the members to save regularly. This is a valuable function of the RoSCA for every participant. It is achieved through the strong social pressure behind the commitment vis-à-vis the group. But there is also another socially valuable function which RoSCA members seem to value highly: In many countries and cultures the participation by individuals in such groups creates a senior claim of the participant on resources that otherwise would have been absorbed by the "sponge" of family needs. Empirical investigations in the informal sector have shown that it is hardly possible to distinguish between the financial affairs of an entrepreneur's family and those of his business. In fact, all aspects of the finances of the family are handled via a single account which absorbs all earnings (cash flow) and from which all outlays are taken (Krahnen/Nitsch, 1987). Therefore, the individual members have little if any opportunity within the family to accumulate savings for some (possibly individual) investment or consumption purpose. Participation in a socially respected institution like a RoSCA thus offers people a way out of the dilemma posed by this family finance system (Schmidt, 1985, p.33).

The transformation of the size of savings is the second function of the RoSCA: Regular savings of an individual over a given span of time lead to a larger amount being available at the end of the saving period. This is in itself a transformation of size. It is valuable if the benefit derived from having the larger amount is larger than the benefit that is forgone by setting aside the payments over time. This benefit of accumulating savings could, for instance, be high if the larger sum can be used to buy a small machine or, more generally, if there is a certain "lumpiness" in the use of funds.

A financial institution like a RoSCA can achieve this advantage of size transformation not only over time but also within a given time period. How this is possible in the case of a RoSCA can only be understood if one takes account of the third function of the RoSCA, which is intermediation: At any time during the cycle there are, economically speaking, group members who are net borrowers and others who are net lenders. So the RoSCA makes it possible – albeit to a very limited extent and for only a short time – to distinguish between the roles of borrower and lender and to realize the benefits offered by this kind of specialization.

Because of intermediation, an enhanced form of size transformation becomes possible in the framework of a RoSCA. Assume the RoSCA consists of 12 women who all want to save in order to buy a sewing machine or new shoes for their children. Saving individually, they would have to set aside their small savings over a period of twelve months until they had enough to buy the machine or the shoes. They would all have to wait for a year before they could buy the desired object – assuming they were able to "protect" their savings for that long. In the RoSCA which meets at the end of every month, not all of them would have to wait. Rather, the woman who receives the "hand" first can buy and use the object after one month, the second woman after two months, etc. So there is a benefit from putting their savings together and temporarily building up net borrower and lender positions. Thus, the second function of size transformation is clearly enhanced by being combined with the third function of intermediation.

But even without its impact on size transformation, the function of intermediation is valuable. Either by arranging the sequence in advance in an appropriate way or by using the auction mechanism, the group can transfer funds from those who need them less urgently or presently have less valuable uses for them to those who need them more urgently or can put them to better use. In other words, by permitting intermediation in the course of the cycle, the social value of the savings of all group members can be increased.

auction mechanism is used for determining who receives the "hand". But this benefit can also be achieved in the most simple form of the RoSCA. Members of the group who face unexpected financial burdens (a child's illness, for example) can "jump the queue" and immediately receive the money in the fund, provided that they have not already been recipients during the cycle that is currently in progress. However, if there is someone else in the group who also needs money urgently, these two members will bid against each other, in which case the auction process may lead to a huge discount. Thus, the size of the insurance premium is not fixed and will vary in accordance with the level of risk to which the other group members are exposed and the urgency of their financial needs.

2.2.2 Evaluation

The benefits of a RoSCA are clearly discernible, and they are apparently very valuable for those who do not have access to a well-functioning formal financial system of banks and insurance companies. Research in all parts of the world shows unambiguously that people want RoSCAs for their benefits, and that they use them (Adams, 1992). But simply pointing out the benefits is not enough to explain why the RoSCA as a group-related institution has been, and still is, found in so many countries and cultures. Why is this so? What makes this type of institution survive? What are the features of a RoSCA which permit it to limit the costs to the members?

The "standard" RoSCA as described above has several features which make it self-stabilizing to a quite remarkable degree (see diagram in Figure 3). These features are created by the interplay between a simple allocation rule, the distribution cycle and a situation characterized by a symmetrical distribution of information. The distribution cycle makes the RoSCA a self-enforcing arrangement. A never-ending sequence of cycles, in which each member takes turns being a saver and a borrower, would create a perfect relationship. In reality RoSCAs may not go through more than one or two cycles. But the social bond which typically exists between RoSCA members functions like a substitute for a never-ending sequence of cycles and prevents members from "defecting" after they have received the sum collected at one meeting.

However, reciprocity has an additional function. It also makes the members willing to engage in "peer-monitoring": every "saver" has a vested interest in seeing to it that the "borrower" puts the funds to sound use and is able to make his/her contribution, i.e. to pay the money back, since he or she is scheduled to be the "borrower" at one of the group's

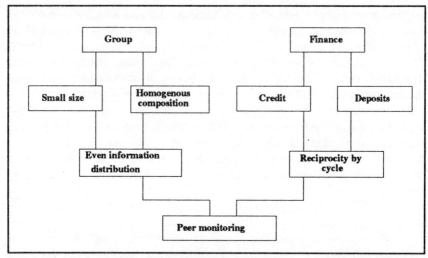

Figure 3:   *Efficient peer–monitoring in the RoSCA through the interplay of an even information distribution and a credible reciprocity relationship.*

meetings in the not–too–distant future. Those who are currently "savers" will not all get their chance to become "borrowers" unless the number of persons paying their predetermined share into the fund, remains the same until such time as the shift from "saver" to "borrower" takes place for each individual who is involved in the process.

The existence of the credit cycle (and thus of the relationship of reciprocity) is one of two necessary prerequisites for the effectiveness of the peer–monitoring mechanism. The other is that, in terms of the information available to the individual members, the group must be in a position to evaluate the creditworthiness of each borrower on an ongoing basis and to determine whether he or she is using the loan in a way that assures future participation in the payment cycle (Stiglitz, 1990). Thus, the individual members must all be more or less equally well informed about those aspects of their fellow members' lives that have a bearing on their "credit rating". This requirement in turn has two implications with respect to the composition of the group. For one thing, it must be of a "manageable" size, i.e. small enough to ensure that each individual member can "keep an eye on" all of his/her fellow members. For another, the members must be similar enough to each other in terms of their social position, place of residence – and perhaps also with respect to their overall life–style and how they earn their livelihood – to make it feasible for them to accurately assess each other's behaviour. If these two preconditions – reciprocity and symmetrical distribution of information – are met, the RoSCA can provide its financial services efficiently.

One additional element which certainly contributes to the popularity and stability of the RoSCA needs to be mentioned. There is no need for the lender/saver to delegate the monitoring function to an officer or manager, as has been explained. Given the way in which a standard RoSCA operates, there is also no need to delegate the treasury function of keeping and managing funds which have been collected. At each meeting the contributions of all members are given to one of them so that there is no money left which could be stolen or embezzled by a dishonest treasurer. There is no need to have a treasurer in the first place, and thus the members need not worry about the honesty of the treasurer and need not find ways of monitoring him/her (Schmidt, 1986).

By using peer-monitoring (and thus by doing without delegated monitoring), the RoSCA minimizes the size of the required administrative "apparatus". It must, however, be borne in mind that there is a trade-off involved here: a high price is paid for this efficiency, which is based on the RoSCA's organizational structure and the incentives which it creates, in so far as it substantially limits the range of financial services which the RoSCA can furnish to its members. This is our fourth question: What are the inherent limitations of the services provided by the RoSCA, and how are these limitations related to the principles of operation of this type of institution?

The fact that reciprocity is an essential prequisite for efficiency means that every member must switch back and forth between the roles of "saver" and "borrower". Accordingly, it is impossible to build up longer-term savings or debt positions. Although reciprocity is a sine qua non of financial intermediation in a RoSCA, it also creates an upper limit for that intermediation. This inherent limitation primarily affects the potential for term transformation. Furthermore, "unscheduled" access by the individual member to his or her savings (i.e. access before it is his or her turn to receive the common fund) is either completely impossible or possible only on potentially unfavourable terms (as in the case of the auction system that provides insurance, as described above). This means that RoSCAs cannot supply their members with one of the essential products offered by financial intermediaries, namely liquidity.

In addition, the small number of members in the group, which is a prerequisite for the effectiveness of peer-monitoring, and the non-contractual commitment to continue to interact socially after the cycle is completed, make it impossible for size transformation to be effected on a major scale. Finally, the group's homogeneous structure, together with its small size, limits the scope for risk diversification among the members. Accordingly, it appears quite probable that a cumulation of risk will occur.

Thus, with respect to all three of the components that make up intermediation – term, size and risk transformation – the potential of a RoSCA is quite limited. By implication, the importance of the above-mentioned service provided by a RoSCA should be borne in mind, namely the fact that the individual members of the group voluntarily enter into a binding agreement with each other which obliges them to save. This is a mechanism which can – and should – be utilized in new financial technologies that are developed for institutions operating in the semiformal and formal sectors. We will discuss this aspect in greater detail in the next chapter.

2.3   Credit Cooperatives

2.3.1   Analytical Description

Finally, since profits are distributed to all of the members of a CC, there is no intrinsic incentive to engage in usurious lending. The ownership structure of the CC effectively and visibly eliminates the motive of rent-seeking on the part of the "owners". This follows from the fact that the "democratic" structure of the CC ensures that any accrued income is distributed equally among all of its members. This may be an important and widely accepted ethical reason for the ubiquity of CCs in many developing countries. The fact that credit allocationCredit cooperatives (CCs) fall into the category of semi-formal financial institutions. They operate within parameters set by the institutions of the legal infrastructure (i.e. they are to some degree subject to monitoring and supervision by government regulatory agencies); they are officially registered; they have a written corporate constitution; and they conduct their operations in accordance with binding, formal rules. CCs may be members of national leagues or federations and of international associations (for example, the World Council of Credit Unions) which represent their political interests. Although a relatively large body of information is available on this type of financing arrangement, there are very few studies of CCs which use an analytical approach in describing them and assessing their potential and limitations (among them are Rasmusen, 1988; Braverman/Guasch, 1989).

In most developing countries, CCs have been set up in two- or three-tier systems which effectively link CCs nationwide. In contrast to the European prototype, CCs in developing countries have typically been established from the "top down" and are closely linked to governmental institutions. Sometimes the Ministry of Finance or a Ministry of

Cooperatives is directly responsible for the regulation of these institutions. Most countries differ somewhat in terms of the precise type of institutional set-up that has been created for CCs, and in the following discussion we will disregard these variations.

What are common and fundamental characteristics of CCs, and how do they operate?

The idea of group solidarity or self-help, which is the basis of cooperative action, implies that members are clients on both sides of the balance sheet. Members provide capital to the CC, which may be equity in the form of shares, and debt in the form of deposits, and they receive loans. At the same time the "clients" are the "owners" as well.

Decisions on matters of fundamental importance can only be taken by the owners of the institution. So, at least in principle, they are made by the entire membership of the cooperative meeting in the general assembly. It is part of the basic notion of a cooperative that all members should have equal voting rights. Furthermore, the equity capital of cooperatives is revocable. Individual members (owners) may decide to leave the cooperative. If this happens, the cooperative buys back the share held by the member in question and he or she receives the par value of the claim. Departing members do not receive any portion of the cooperative's financial reserves or accumulated profits. Thus, the question of how profits are distributed among the various interest groups within the cooperative – namely, the borrowers, the lenders, the owners and the management – is an interesting one. As members are typically borrowers, lenders, and owners, the question can be rephrased as follows: How are profits distributed among members in their various roles on the one side and the management on the other side?

Three modes of distribution can be distinguished. First, distribution may be according to the volume of business transacted with the individual member in question. The volume of business per member may be measured on the deposit side, on the loan side, or both. An example of profit distribution according to loan business transacted is the policy of interest reimbursement. Second, there is distribution according to equity shares. In this case, profits are distributed as dividends. Third, profits may not be distributed at all – in other words, they may be retained and reinvested, e.g. via lending to the members. For the sake of completeness, a fourth alternative should also be mentioned. This is an "informal" mode of distribution which implies on-the-job-consumption of profits by the management or, more generally, the administrative staff of the cooperative. Since a certain limited opportunity to use funds belonging to the cooperative for their own purposes is one of the management's fringe benefits, this mode of distribution is in fact an outgrowth of the agency problem between members and management, as will be discussed below.

Surprisingly, there is almost no systematic empirical evidence on modes of profit distribution in existing CCs in any part of the developing world. For some industrialized countries it has been clearly demonstrated that retaining earnings is the principal mode of using surpluses in CCs (Bonus/Schmidt, 1990, p. 181).

We will now address the question of which financial services a CC can provide. First of all, a CC provides opportunities for members to save and thus to accumulate wealth, and it also permits borrowing. This implies size transformation for the individual member and the group as a whole, and financial intermediation: Some members can establish net borrower positions while others can be net savers or lenders. Qualitatively, there is no difference between the benefits derived from these services and those obtained from the services provided by a RoSCA. But there are enormous quantitative differences, as the scope of individual capital accumulation, size transformation and intermediation is not limited by any formal reciprocity requirement or cycle mechanism. The implication of this is that net surplus positions (deposits/share holding) and net deficit positions (loans) can be built up and held over a long period of time. This enables each member to determine the type and extent of his or her individual net position based on needs, preferences and investment opportunities, and it permits the group and its members to fully reap the benefit of specializing in the roles of saver and investor.

The fact that there are no organizational constraints which limit the size of the net positions which the members may seek to establish vis-à-vis the CC does not imply that there are also no financial constraints. Obviously, the CC cannot lend out more than its members save and deposit. It also does not imply that reciprocity is not important and that some members would not want to change their position from net lender to net borrower. But what is important is this: the institution does not make it an operational principle that savers become borrowers, and vice-versa, according to a predetermined pattern.

Because it in principle offers unlimited intermediation, and because members are able to determine their net financial positions according to their own needs and wishes, a CC can also provide the very valuable service of term or maturity transformation: Different members can hold deposits for a shorter term than the term or maturity of the loans granted because the deposits which some member may withdraw can be replaced by new deposits coming form other members. So the CC provides, at least to some extent, the service of liquidity.

Due to their principles of operation, CCs may have a large number of members. Indeed, the potential for intermediation and size transformation grows with the number of members. A large membership makes another service or function possible: risk transformation. For the CC as a whole, the diversification of assets, e.g. across occupations and areas of economic activity, is feasible if there are a large number of members and if the membership is heterogeneous. Comparatively risky loans can thus be transformed into less risky deposits.

In a large CC, peer–monitoring cannot play an important role, and it is necessary to have a management which may be recruited from among the members or from outside. Peer–monitoring is substituted by delegated monitoring.

All in all, a CC is very much like a bank. But there are two benefits which it offers its members that a bank cannot offer its customers. Due to the fact that the cooperative is owned by the same group of people from whom it obtains funds (depositors) and to whom it extends credit (borrowers), the process of financial intermediation is limited to the region where the owners live. At least in principle, financial flows cannot easily be directed out of the region where the CC operates. This regional bias has been one of the major reasons for the successful evolution of cooperative banks in Germany, for example. Financial institutions which are not organized as cooperatives always tend to redistribute funds on an interregional basis. This may lead to a systematic drain of capital from the outlying regions of the country (peripherial areas) to the central areas (capital). In the history of many developing countries, including the history of Germany in the last century, the asymmetry of savings and credit opportunities has always been an important issue. It should be noted that the principle of intraregional intermediation applies even if there are substantial interest differentials between the outlying regions and urban areas. Thus, in a financial system that includes CCs, a positive interest differential between the centre and the periphery is not sufficient to draw funds from the peripheral areas to the centre. CCs thus help to insulate a regional economy from the temptations of short–term profitability in those areas of the country that are already industrialized. Hence, the "intraregional principle", which makes regional economies relatively insular and is nowadays seen as a drawback in most industrialized countries, may be interpreted as an important asset in developing is not associated with a personal relationship of dependence which can be created when people are in debt to a moneylender may well increase the confidence of the general public in the integrity of the financial relationship.

2.3.2 Evaluation

After focussing on the services which the CC can offer, we now turn to the question of how efficiently it can provide them. It is important to remember here that the efficiency of its operations as a financial intermediary will be influenced by the incentive structures which are established and maintained by the cooperatives's corporate constitution for both its members and its management staff.

Of particular importance in this context is the design of the owners' property rights that are granted to the members of the cooperative. When discussing the owners' property rights in the case of cooperatives, the following three features are emphasized as typical, defining characteristics: the equity capital is revocable; it is bought back at the nominal (face) value; and the property rights grant to the member quasi-democratic rights to participate in decision–making processes.

Whether becoming/being a member of a cooperative is an attractive proposition or not will depend on the benefits associated with membership. Obviously, these benefits will be determined by the services provided by the CC, as discussed above, and by the method by which they are distributed (and granted) to members. But there is another important aspect here which is far from being obvious: The ownership rights in turn determine which services and how many benefits are there to be distributed. The most important "channel of influence" goes through the management, as is shown in Figure 4 on the next page: All rights of all owners jointly determine how decisions can and will be made. That is, they determine the range of activities among which the managers can choose, and the incentive structure that determines how they would want to use this scope of action. So, in the final analysis, ownership rights determine how managers determine the benefits that are to be distributed in a specified way.

Because the owners can redeem their shares in the cooperative, the institution faces the risk that members will withdraw equity capital, either individually or in large numbers. This in turn means that the capital base that is available for financial activities, and more importantly for risk bearing, is not safeguarded. This threat to the very existence of the cooperative explains why the management is strongly motivated to secure its position by creating an internal capital base. It can easily do so by retaining earnings. The willingness on the part of management to use internal financing is also fostered by the second feature that was pointed out above. Shares of the cooperative's equity capital are repurchased at their nominal value. There is only a primary market, and not a secondary market, for the cooperative's shares. Accordingly, the market value of a share is the same as the nominal value, i.e. it is not equal to a fraction of the cooperative's net worth (assets minus liabilities). Since profits and reserves accumulated by the enterprise are not reflected in an increase in the value of its stock, purchasing shares in a cooperative is an unattractive

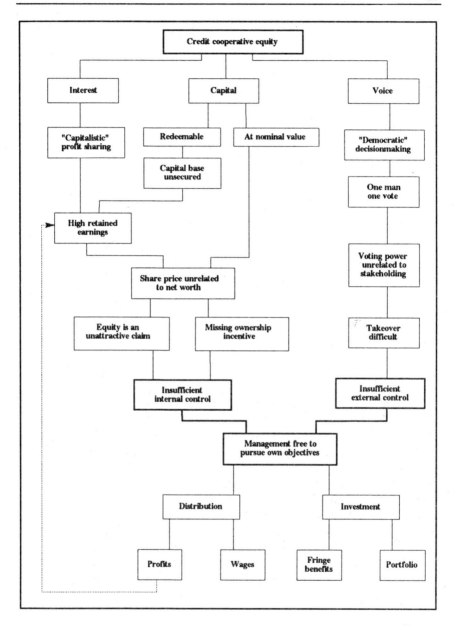

Figure 4: *The corporate constitution of the Credit Cooperative systematically weakens incentives for internal as well as external control, giving considerable discretionary powers to the employee-managers. As a result, the investment and*

*distribution decisions taken by credit cooperatives are likely to
be suboptimal.*

investment option. As external equity financing is made difficult by this
fact, the CC, and particularly its management, is all the more willing to
create a capital base by means of internal financing.

But this in turn means that, to a considerable degree, financial
decisions made by the credit cooperative are no longer contingent upon
the provision of capital inflows on a certain scale by the members, and can
thus be taken without regard for the opinions and wishes of the members.

The fact that the value of the cooperative's shares is not linked to its
net worth also has an impact on the willingness of the members to take an
active part in its affairs and to identify with it as an institution. Thus, in the
vast majority of cases the general assembly does not really perform the
functions of a "parliament" expressing and safeguarding the interests of
the members. However, this means that the power which (in formal
terms) resides with the members in their capacity as owners of the
cooperative is not in fact exercised by them due to a lack of incentives
that would motivate them to feel and act like owners. In the final analysis,
the members' lack of identification with their role as owners means that it
is indeed impossible for them to monitor the actions of the institution's
management and apply sanctions in cases of poor performance or
wrongdoing.

If one cannot expect internal control to be exercised in a CC, it is
worth asking whether external control mechanisms exist – for example, of
the type that can be created when a small group of active owners gains
control of voting rights (and thus oversight rights) that are not being
used. A situation of this kind, which is sometimes called a "takeover" in
countries with developed capital markets, cannot arise in a CC due to the
democratic decision–making processes which are a typical feature of
cooperatives. Each member has exactly one vote at the "shareholders'
meetings" and, as a result, an individual member who might accumulate a
sizeable financial stake in the corporation could never acquire a block of
votes proportionate to the size of his or her stockholding. As has already
been pointed out, the fact that power in terms of voting rights is not a
function of a given member's share of the institution's equity capital
means that even if someone acquired a majority of the capital, he or she
could never "take over" the cooperative. The resulting lack of external
control will obviously strengthen the autonomy of management vis-à-vis
the members of the CC.

The freedom of action enjoyed by the management of a cooperative
due to the lack of both internal and external control is further increased

by the above-mentioned lack of dependence on financial resources from external sources. So there are a total of three factors which are responsible for the large degree of autonomy which characterizes the role of a cooperative's management in terms of defining its objectives and the institution's business policy.

This brings us to two important questions: If the management staff is largely free to run the cooperative as they like, what goals will they pursue? And if they pursue their own objectives, is this good or bad for the members and conducive or detrimental to the survival of "their" CC?

The main interest of management is probably in preserving the security of their jobs and their income in a broad sense. This income comprises not only the salary and other financial benefits but also non-pecuniary forms of income such as social prestige, favourable working conditions, business trips, etc. Note that, due to the lack of monitoring, this income derived from a management position in a CC can be higher than the income which could be achieved in other positions. Income in this sense is a stream over time, it can only be enjoyed as long as the CC exists.

The managers have no opportunity to sell their future income stream from the CC in the capital market. Therefore they are not interested in maximizing the present value of this stream. Because there is no secondary market in which CC managers could sell CC shares at their intrinsic or economic value, they also have no incentive to maximize profits or the market value of the CC shares. So the managers of a CC will not behave in the way in which the owners (members) would prefer them to behave if the CC were a stock-corporation with publicly traded shares. There appears to be a conflict between shareholder and manager interests.

Since the manager's income is a stream to be enjoyed over time, the behaviour of the management will be based on the principle of "safety first". The members of the management staff will do all they can to safeguard their jobs, and thus their "moderately too high" income streams. They will let options pass by if they are somewhat risky, even if members as owners would not want them to do so. In particular, they will follow an "excessively" cautious lending policy (Rasmusen, 1988). As long as managers do not go too far in pursuing this policy, members cannot do anything about it because they do not know about it – or, more precisely, because they have no incentive to find out about it.

However, a policy of overly cautious credit extension also has advantages for members because it implies that members in their capacity as depositors enjoy a high degree of protection. Thus, in a CC with a largely autonomous and self-seeking (and clever) management, the

interests of members as depositors take precedence over the interests of
members as owners and as borrowers.

How important is this tendency towards a safety–oriented policy of
CCs, which has the effect of undermining and weakening incentives to
manage the CCs efficiently? The answer depends on the quality of the
entire banking system. As is well known, the principal threat to the safety
of deposits at privately owned commercial banks arises from the fact that,
from time to time, these banks are willing to make risky investments.
Requirements set by regulatory agencies with regard to capital adequacy
standards for banks and the maintenance of a minimum level of diversification in their lending business are designed above all to limit the level
of risk to which these institutions – due to the incentive system in private
banks – are exposed via their loan portfolios. The governance structure of
CCs thus appears particularly suitable for an environment in which
additional external monitoring mechanisms to ensure the safety of
savings deposits (for example, those of a national banking supervisory
authority) either do not exist or do not function well.

The conflict between efficiency in credit decisions and preserving the
safety of savers' capital – i.e. the necessity of opting for extremely low–
risk investments, and thus sacrificing profitability, in order to provide a
high degree of depositor protection – becomes less and less important the
more likely it becomes that a given financial institution's business policy
will be subject to external monitoring. Whether such external monitoring
mechanisms are available may be a function of the level of development of
the financial market as a whole, because effective competition on the
deposit and credit market is just another type of external control.

It is important to remember that, particularly in those countries (e.g.
Germany) in which the credit cooperatives have played an important role
historically – and in which they have been in operation for more than a
century – they were not subject to any visible form of external monitoring
in the initial years of their existence (Bonus/Schmidt, 1990). The fact that
they were able to convince savers that they pursued a prudent investment
policy may thus have been an important reason for the early success of
the cooperatives movement. The more recent experience with CCs in
developing countries confirms our findings: CCs are widespread, they
rarely fail, and they are most often very conservative, "stagnant" financial
institutions which do not grow. Their inherent conservatism is one reason
why they have survived for so long even though they are inefficient[6].

---

[6]   See among others Marion, 1987; WOCCU, 1988; Huppi/Feder, 1990; Magill,
1991

2.3.3 Some Remarks on Multipurpose Cooperatives

In the cooperatives sector, financial services – in particular credit facilities – are supplied not only by credit cooperatives but also by Multipurpose Cooperatives (MPCs). The lending operations of MPCs are of particular interest from the standpoint of credit technology because it would seem logical to assume that their activities in the various areas in which they operate are complementary – in other words, that the interplay and "overlap" between them enhances the efficiency and profitability of their business in each field – and that these "synergies" are consciously exploited by MPCs. In the ongoing discussion of target–group–oriented financing options and credit–delivery systems, the view is occasionally expressed (Armbruster, 1990) that MPCs are thus in a position to use a contractual structure which originated in the informal financial sector and which is used quite consciously and to considerable advantage by the institutions operating in that sector – namely interlinked transactions (see Chapter C). With a contractual setup of this type, which is frequently explained using the example of a landowner and his tenant (who may be a sharecropper), several different business relationships are linked in an intelligent way to form a single overall arrangement. The quality and viability of each of the individual components of this network of relationships are supposed to be enhanced by their mutual interaction.

Let us illustrate this idea by elaborating the concrete example of a landlord and his tenant, assuming that these two persons conclude two separate contracts, namely an input sales contract (fertilizer), and a credit contract. If the landlord is shrewd when it comes to determining the relationship between the fertilizer price and the loan terms, he can encourage the tenant to make more intensive use of fertilizer by charging a lower price. Doing so will in turn increase the likelihood that the loan will be repaid. Obviously, it only makes sense to sell the fertilizer to the tenant on favourable terms if this increases the probability that the loan will be paid back. As a result, the landlord can sell the fertilizer at a lower price than other potential suppliers or may be able to offer more favourable loan terms than other potential lenders. In this sense, the two contracts are interlinked and efficiency–increasing.

Does this principle apply in the case of an MPC? We think that it is quite doubtful whether the efficiency–enhancing effects of interlinked contracts can also be achieved by MPCs. The reason is this: While the landlord is obviously pursuing a single objective in both contractual relationships that he enters into – namely, maximization of the profit he makes by interacting with his tenant – it cannot be assumed that such a congruence of objectives will exist within an enterprise whose affairs are managed by an administrative apparatus and in which authority for entire areas of its operations may be delegated to specialists within that apparatus. Indeed, if we consider a situation which is analogous to the one in our landlord/tenant example, it is quite conceivable that both the input supply department and the credit department of a cooperative will simultaneously pursue widely differing goals (e.g. maximization of the number of employees, maximization of sales). In such a situation, it would presumably be very difficult, if not impossible, to achieve an optimal coordination and "harmonization" of the contractual terms that define the various parts of the overall business relationship between the cooperative and the customer.

Furthermore, different departments of one and the same cooperative may pursue goals that are mutually incompatible. Each department may be striving to maximize the profitability of its operations, with no consideration being given to any detrimental, profit–reducing side effects that may impinge upon the activities of other departments. The price of the fertilizer is likely to be set without taking into account its impact on the probability of loan repayment.

In addition, MPCs presumably also face the same immense internal and external monitoring problems that were outlined above in our discussion of credit cooperatives; indeed, these problems are probably even more serious at MPCs. The magnitude of these monitoring problems, in conjunction with the often strong influence exerted on MPCs by a ministry of cooperatives or some other ministry, may serve to widen still more the gap between the goals pursued by the enterprise and the actual objectives of its members. There is a danger that MPCs in particular will be co–opted by the government administrative apparatus – as evidenced, for example, by the fact that they are frequently used as a vehicle for state intervention in the markets for agricultural products. This, of course, makes it even less likely that these cooperatives will serve the interests of their owner–members. Furthermore, the administrative links with the government and its executive agencies – which are often utilized as instruments of repression and/or taxation – create an overall environment in which it is difficult for the institution to identify with – and cater for the needs of – the target group.

2.4 Group Lending

2.4.1 Analytical Description

Following the famous example of the Grameen Bank (Hossain, 1988) and the activities of ACCION (Otero, 1986, 1988), tying several borrowers to each other through the formation of borrower groups has become a common practice in credit extension to small and informal–sector enterprises, especially among NGOs.

How does group lending work? Usually the group is formed for the sole purpose of receiving loans from some outside source. All paperwork necessary for obtaining the loan (or loans) is then jointly completed by the members of the group. The financial institution providing loans is separate from the group, and it operates in either the formal or the semi–formal financial sector. Loans may be extended to all group members individually or they may be given to the group as a whole. Similarily, the liability may be assigned to individual members or it may be assigned to the group in its entirety (joint and several liability). Also, there are some programmes that require group members to make an initial savings deposit in order to be eligible to receive credit. Often these savings deposits are frozen and used as collateral for the loans.

Essentially, all group members are net borrowers. This is in contrast to the RoSCA, where each group member is both a borrower and a lender, and to the credit cooperative where, at any point in time, some group members are borrowers, while others are lenders. The typical borrower in a group lending scheme has to pay interest to the lender, who is not part of the group.

What is the function or service or benefit of group lending for those who belong to the groups?

Being able to join a borrowers' group is very valuable to members if this is the only way for them to get access to loans on reasonable terms. Thus, the benefit of group lending is derived from the benefit of getting a loan. The latter may be very great, and thus the groups may be very valuable for their members. In addition, borrowing in the framework of a group may substantially reduce transaction costs for the borrowers.

Why would some lenders consider granting loans to certain people only if they are members of borrowers' groups? One reason is the high cost of lending small sums to people who are extremely poor and who have neither a credit record nor collateral. Forming and using groups of borrowers is assumed to result in transaction–cost economies for the lender. And it also appears that group lending can reduce the risks of lending. So it is conceivable that the offer to extend loans in the framework of a group lending scheme is the only acceptable (i.e. affordable) financing offer that is made to certain target groups by the semi–formal and formal financial sectors.

It should be noted that some of the cost economies for the lender and some of the risk reduction simply result from the shifting of costs and risks onto the individual borrower or to the groups. Therefore, with respect to costs and risks, group lending may not be more attractive from the point of view of the borrower than applying for a loan on an individual

64

basis. However, this comparison is only relevant if he or she has a real chance of getting an individual loan on terms that would otherwise be comparable to those offered in conjunction with the group lending arrangement.

2.4.2 Evaluation

In spite of the apparent similarities to RoSCAs and credit cooperatives, it is important to bear in mind that "group lending" is not a type of financial institution. Rather, it is a method or tool that can be used by financial institutions that wish to lend to very poor customers but at the same time limit the costs and risks which they incur by doing so. Indeed, the concept of group lending was developed by banks and NGOs/PVOs for that purpose.

As in the case of the RoSCA, two conditions have to be met in order for group lending to function efficiently: peer-monitoring and reciprocity must be given. Peer-monitoring is the supervision of the behaviour of one group member by other group members. It is feasible only if group members are able to observe and evaluate the conduct of other group members as far as credit use and repayment is concerned. This requires that the groups be small and socially homogeneous. Reciprocity is created by making the borrowers assume joint liability or, in a weaker form, by making access to further loans to the group or its members contingent on compliance with repayment terms by all group members. Both forms of reciprocity create an incentive for all group members to monitor their peers within the group and even to help them repay or to apply social pressure to force them to do so.

At least in principle, group lending can reduce risks by increasing the ability and the willingness of individual borrowers to repay loans, just as, in principle, the transaction costs can be reduced. However, these benefits are not net benefits. Group lending creates additional risks and additional transaction costs: Additional risks arise from the possibility that the groups might fail to function, and the costs of establishing the groups have to be considered as additional transaction costs of lending. It is not at all clear whether in the majority of cases the reductions in repayment risk and transaction costs in lending are sufficient to offset the additional risk of failing groups and the costs of forming and maintaining groups. Experience shows that only very successful group lending schemes achieve a net reduction of risks and costs. In the majority of cases, the expected reduction of total or net risks and costs does not materialize (Boomgard, 1989; Holt, 1991a; Rhyne, 1991; Rhyne/Otero, 1991).

The financial performance of group lending schemes is subject to three important constraints: (1) the scope for transaction-cost economies is in fact quite limited; (2) their capacity for risk-sharing is low; and (3) collusion and "free-riding" among group members could "undermine" the entire collective repayment process.

First, there is a positive correlation between the size of the group and the scope for achieving transaction-cost economies. This is obvious because most of the above-mentioned costs are fixed costs. Therefore, the average transaction cost level per group member is inversely related to the size of the group. However, there is a negative correlation between the size of the groups and the effectiveness of peer-monitoring. Hence, a trade-off between transaction-cost economies and peer-monitoring economies has to be taken into account. As a result, the group membership has to be restricted, which in turn limits the scope for transaction-cost economies. To give an example, the Grameen Bank in Bangladesh, which some authors consider to be one of the most important financial innovations of the recent past, has limited its group size to five members (Hossain, 1988). Obviously, only very limited transaction-cost economies can be realized here.

Second, what increases the effectiveness of peer-monitoring reduces the scope for risk sharing. Both the potential for effective peer-monitoring and the feasibility of risk sharing are a function of the homogeneity of the group. Greater homogeneity increases the effectiveness of peer-monitoring simply because peers know more about each other if they are all more or less alike. On the other hand, though, homogeneity might make it more difficult to diversify overall economic risk within the group. Hence, effective peer-monitoring due to a homogeneous group structure might expose the group as a whole to a considerable amount of economic risk which could have been diversified away through the formation of a heterogeneous group made up of people exposed to different types of risk in their economic activities.

Third, the fact that the members of the group assume joint liability for the debt – or some economic equivalent of joint liability – might make the decision for or against loan repayment a strategic one that is taken by all borrowers. The possibility of collusion cannot be ruled out. The reason is simple: joint liability vis-à-vis the lender leads in effect to highly correlated repayment decisions on the part of the individual borrowers (and group members). Obviously, nobody in a credit group will want to repay a loan if he or she expects other members to default, because if this happens he/she will in any case be denied access to additional credit(s). In other words, repaying a loan when other members of the group do not is simply not rational. Hence, one would expect to find that either everybody or nobody pays back the money they have received in group lending schemes. This is born out in reality.

Note that group lending also involves an important element of delegated monitoring. It results from the fact that the lending institution delegates the task of monitoring borrowers to the group. But it cannot completely avoid monitoring the functioning and coherence of the group. In any case, though, the intensity with which the credit–extending institution will monitor the behaviour of the borrower group cannot be accurately assessed until one has examined not only the incentive structure that has been created for the group by the lending institution, but also the nature of the relationship that exists between this institution, e.g. a local NGO, and the ultimate provider of the funds, e.g. a donor institution in an industrialized country. Accordingly, group lending – defined as the peer–monitoring component of a larger financing arrangement of this type – is only one part of the financial relationship that must be analysed in its entirety.

2.5   Towards a Comparative Analysis of Group-Oriented Financial Institutions

Having discussed different types of informal and semi–formal institutions, we must now address the question of how a comparative evaluation of financial institutions can be performed. As the following considerations mainly serve the purpose of demonstrating the method of a comparative analysis, they are restricted to the genuine types of institutions, i.e. the RoSCA and the credit cooperative (CC). Our above analysis may be summarized by citing two criteria which are applied to both types of institutions, namely their potential in terms of financial intermediation (financial efficiency) and, on the other, the efficiency with which the relevant financial services would be performed (organizational efficiency). In banking, three different types of transformation are usually distinguished that jointly define the term intermediation: size transformation, term transformation (and thus the production of liquidity), and risk transformation (i.e. diversification, control, and information production). The first step in a comparative analysis consists in evaluating the institutions being studies in terms of these two efficiency measures. The application of this method is summarized in Table 3.

While each of the two types of institution provides all three kinds of transformation, the RoSCA is only capable of performing these services on a very limited scale. The reason for this is the small size of the groups that are involved – which, however, must be kept small in order to ensure the effectiveness of reciprocity and of peer–monitoring. By contrast, the ability

	Financial Potential (Extent of transformation)			Organizational Potential (Monitoring incentive)	
Criteria	Size transformation	Liquidity	Risk diversi-fication	Monitoring	Incentives
RoSCA	limited (by group size)	limited (to auction type RoSCAs)	limited (by group homogeneity)	Peer-monitoring	Efficient incentives and structure (for small homogenous groups)
Credit Cooperative	unlimited	unlimited	unlimited	Delegated monitoring	Inefficient incentive structure (inconsistent property rights)

Table 3:   *Comparative analysis of financial intermediaries*

of the CC to carry out lot size transformation is not subject to any limitations because the size of its membership is not subject to any inherent restrictions.

With respect to term transformation as well, the potential of the CC is theoretically unlimited. The RoSCA, on the other hand, can perform term transformation only on a very limited scale because loan maturities are necessarily very short in the rotating credit cycle.

The RoSCA also leaves much to be desired as far as risk transformation is concerned. Due to the homogeneity of the group of participants – which is, however, a necessary prerequisite for effective peer-monitoring – its loan portfolio cannot be highly diversified. Moreover, the RoSCA's ability to provide its members with additional liquidity to deal with unforeseen emergencies appears to be very limited. In other words, the institution cannot really offer "financial insurance" to the members of the group. By contrast, the CC can build up a well-diversified portfolio and thus reduce risk effectively. The only constraints to which it is subject in this respect are those that result from its adherence to the "intraregional principle" (capital flows are not directed out of the region served by the cooperative). In addition, the CC is able to produce liquidity by transforming assets that tend to be rather illiquid into short-term deposits.

As regards the second evaluation criterion, that of organizational efficiency, the two intermediaries differ as well. The RoSCA can be regarded as a useful and efficient institution of the informal sector which is established by its members for the purpose of exploiting the advantages offered by peer–monitoring. As an institution, it exhibits a high degree of internal stability.

By contrast, the CC must be characterized as an institution which, from the point of view of its clients, operates according to the principle of blind faith. In practice, the management is not subject to any form of effective supervision (i.e. monitoring by any persons or bodies other than itself). Indeed, in the framework of delegated monitoring as it is necessarily practised in a cooperative, the principal (delegator), the owners and depositors, have to a great extent lost their ability to supervise and, if necessary, discipline the agent, i.e. the management.

As far as the question of monitoring is concerned, what distinguishes the group lending option is its reliance on a combination of the mechanisms used by the two financial institutions, namely delegated monitoring and peer–monitoring. But as explained above group lending cannot be properly analysed unless one knows who the lending institutions and the ultimate provider of capital are, and can assess their motives for providing credit to the target group. Thus, the scope of the analysis must be expanded to include more than just the borrower group. If this is done it immediately becomes clear that the lending institution's motives for pursuing the policy it has selected are an outgrowth of its specific governance structure.

3. Other Types of Unconventional "Financial Institutions": a Brief Overview

This section discusses very briefly three types of providers of financial services which are not banks in the usual sense, and thus appear to be particularly attractive to those experts who are generally reluctant to "believe in banks" as a relevant solution to the problems involved in providing financial services to poor people.

3.1 Revolving Credit Funds

A Revolving Credit Fund (RCF) is simply a stock of capital or a sum of money which has been given to a person or an institution by some donor with the idea that this money can be lent to members of the target group, recovered, lent once more, recovered again, etc. For donors, RCFs appear to be an easy and cost–effective way to reach really poor target groups without having to build up a complicated administrative structure. There are thousands of defunct RCFs in the developing world which have long since ceased to operate because the funds did not flow back from the borrowers.

In terms of their institutional set–up, some RCFs are free–standing, others are attached to a given institution in a developing country, often an NGO, and most frequently they are attached to a larger development project such as an integrated rural development project or an enterprise development project. For the latter case, the project staff – whose principal task is usually not the operation of a micro–scale financial institution – is usually free to decide precisely how the funds are to be used. The idea behind these "appendix RCFs" is that they should help the target population of the main project make use of the opportunities which this project attempts to create.

The financial services provided by the RCF are limited in size and scope. Typically credit is only granted for specific purposes. These purposes are not necessarily those for which the potential clientele would demand credit, but rather what best supports the larger project that is to be complemented by the RCF. Although there is little systematic evidence available on the performance of RCFs (see, however, ILO, 1991), it is an undisputed and widely held belief that RCFs usually run out of money quickly. Our own – admittedly unsystematic – observations indicate that the funds in the capital stock rarely "revolve" more than two times.

The limited lifetime of RCFs is sometimes justified by stating that they are only intended to provide an initial liquidity push for the borrowers. From an economist's point of view, however, the expected impact of such a one–shot credit on productive investment is at best minimal. That would be the case if borrowers where wise enough to anticipate the RCF's limited existence and did not use the loan on irreversible investments. And the impact may even be negative if borrowers expanded their productive facilities, thereby making themselves dependent on an uninterrupted credit supply from the RCF which is, in fact, not forthcoming.

The major reason for the short life of a fund and its limited impact on the target groups is simple. The RCF is not itself the project. Rather, it is established as a temporary instrument for a short–term adjustment period. Although there is nothing wrong with temporary assistance in general, the apparent confusion regarding the nature of the financial support being provided – is it a grant or a loan? – on the part of both the RCF's management and the customers is likely to create a powerful negative effect that will severly limit the development impact and the value for the borrowers. Indeed, an RCF operating with donated loanable funds could and should be considered as an integral part of the financial system of the respective developing country.

The intrinsic financial fragility of the RCF is caused by its organisational inefficiency, which is in turn an outgrowth of its incomplete governance structure. The RCF is set up without defining an ultimate "owner" of the capital, i.e. a person or an institution that will have an incentive to stabilize the fund and to maintain the value of the capital stock. From an economic point of view, an RCF is a mini-bank and not a grant-distributing agency. If it is desired that an RCF is in fact viable this requires that it be set up and run just like an autonomous financial institution. However, if an RCF were in fact run in this way it might lose much of its attractiveness from the point of view of those who would want to use it as play-money, namely the staff of the larger development project.

The case of RCFs given to, and administered by, an NGO may be somewhat less problematic if the NGO develops the ability and the willingness to "defend" the RCF and to preserve its benefits for those borrowers who have to wait until credit is available for them. Some NGOs have been successful in this respect. But the majority has failed probably because there were neither control from the donor, from the intended beneficiaries or from any supervisory institution, nor sanctions for the case that the funds turn out to be lost. The practice at several donor institutions gives reasons to believe that for them it is, indeed, the easiest "solution" if the money is lost quickly. As in many other cases of failing finance projects the basic reason for failure is the lack of incentives to be careful!

3.2 Credit Guarantee Funds

Many observers who have had no experience with a Credit Guarantee Fund (CGF) or a Credit Guarantee System (CGS) tend to expect very much from this instrument of financing small-scale enterprises. But the performance to date of the existing CGFs and CGSs has been largely unimpressive (Levitsky/Prasad, 1986). What are the functions and the potential of CGFs/CGSs and what are the problems involved in establishing and running such institutions?

In essence, a CGS is a kind of insurance company. It covers the risks of the banks whose customers default on their obligations. Looked at from the standpoint of the individual bank with a borrower in default, the loss is shifted to the other banks who pay their premiums without demanding payments from the CGS. Looked at from the standpoint of all the banks employing the CGS, the risk is reduced by diversification, and the uncertain outcome – loss or no loss – is transformed into a (nearly) certain outcome, namely the average loss. This average, or expected, loss as well as the administrative costs, have to be covered by the premiums if the CGS is to survive. Like an insurance policy covering, for example, car accidents, a CGS also increases risks – i.e. the average loss – because it lessens the incentives for the banks to take their own risk reducing measures. This effect is called "moral hazard". For any interval of time actual loses may be larger than the expected or average loss. The residual risk of losses exceeding the premiums charged is borne by the CGS. A credit guarantee fund (in the strict sense of term) is much like a CGS with the sole exception that a certain sum of money, the fund, is "pledged" and put into a blocked account. This money can be utilized to cover a possible excess of losses over premiums. This set–up implies that the residual risk is borne by those who own the CGF.

A CGS/CGF which attempts to cover costs and losses via premiums is similar not only to an insurance company, but also to a bank because a bank, by its very nature, also performs insurance functions: it shifts risks when it charges risk premiums as part of the interest rate, it reduces risk by diversification and it creates "moral hazard", and it bears the residual risk. The essential question is whether a CGS/CGF is in a better position than a bank to shift, reduce, limit and bear the risks involved in granting credit to small firms, farms und households. The *general answer* to this question is that the bank, and not the CGS/CGF, is the more efficient institutional mechanism, because it can – and it is clearly motivated to – limit the factor of "moral hazard" to a larger extent. Besides, banks often have more diversified portfolios, and leaving the residual risk with the bank avoids a duplication of administrative costs (cf. Zeitinger/Schmidt, 1984).

Due to the effect of diversification, the amount of credit insured by a CGS/CGF could be considerably larger than the sum of money in the fund. This is the multiplier effect. It only functions if there is somebody who accepts the risk that the aggregate losses will exceed the amount in the fund. A simple CGS/CGF has a multiplier effect if and only if banks do not require complete coverage of their loans. In reality banks are often not prepared to bear any risks. Thus, it does not make much difference whether a certain amount of money is put into a CGF in order to cover the risk of bank loans at 100% or whether the same amount is simply lent out as a credit fund.

The comparison above may seem unfair because banks deal with what they would consider to be risky borrowers by simply not granting credits to them. In contrast, it is the explicit purpose of CGSs/CGFs to induce banks to increase their lending to poor target–groups by accepting risks which the banks would not accept. This purpose can in fact be fulfilled as long as the CGS/CGF does not want or does not need to break even in the long run. Indeed, most CGSs all over the world are so heavily subsidized by their respective governments or by other sponsors that they need not cover costs and losses. And most CGFs simply decapitalize in a short time because they do not manage to avoid deficits. Subsidies as well as institutions which cannot survive are, however, of doubtful value to the target groups.

There are two situations in which a CGS/CGF can help small enterprises, farms and households, and still survive. One is the "ideal case" that banks would want to work with these borrowers but shy away from it because they overestimate the riskiness of small loans. In this case, a CGS/CGF can function and survive because it corrects an error on the banks' side. This advantage may even be large enough to counterbalance the genuine disadvantages of a CGS/CGF mentioned above. The other case is that the local banking system is extremely inefficient. A CGS/CGF might, in this case, introduce a new element into the banking system which could eventually result in more small-scale loans. Both these situations are, however, not likely to obtain in the real world.

In sum, a CGF may be a useful instrument of small-scale financing. But it is highly improbable that this will be the case. The inherent drawbacks of the concept of a CGS/CGF are very hard to overcome, and the practical problems of running a CGS/CGF are equally serious. A CGF is only useful if banks lack experience and know-how in the area of small-scale lending and at the same time behave cooperatively – but in this case direct support of the relevent banks would seem to be easier and more effective.

3.3 Post Office Savings Banks

Post Office Savings Banks, which can be found in several African and Asian countries, are financial institutions of a peculiar nature. Almost without exception, they are only entitled to accept deposits, and not to lend, and often they still are a part of the postal service. In recent years, some of them have formally been made independent of their respective postal system, but more or less keep operating through the post offices. That is, customers make deposits or withdrawals at their local post offices. Almost always, a POSB must pass all or a large fraction of the funds which are being mobilized to the Treasury of the country.

The economic and developmental role of POSBs is ambivalent. As financial intermediaries they channel funds from the general – and mostly poor – population to the government, a function which will not generally be regarded as conducive to development. However, as providers of financial services they are indeed able to offer the valuable deposit service even in the remotest parts of the country. The fact that POSBs have originally been set up by governments, most often even by former colonial administrations, for the purpose of mobilizing cheap funds from the people has always been the true reason why the POSBs were, and still are, not allowed to enter the lending business irrespective of the question whether they are qualified to act as lenders. The interest of the respective Treasury is only mildly hidden behind the rhetoric found in POSB–laws and proclamations that these institutions serve the purpose of "thrift promotion". Nevertheless, the government interest in cheap credit and the people's interest in easily accessible deposit facilities may be compatible in the case of POSBs. That is the reason why they are interesting from a development perspective in the first place.

At least in principle, the deposit service offered by a POSB is valuable for the poorer segments of the population. As is well known, in countries with poorly developed financial markets, and, in particular, an under-developed market for formal insurance, providing oneself with financial reserves is one of the most important savings motives. Many households save simply in order to have cash at hand in case of unexpected events such as accidents or illness. Thus, in order to meet the needs of persons who see savings primarily as a form of insurance, a savings programme must offer a high degree of safety in order to prevent losses as a result of theft or accidents and quick accessibility in order to guarantee liquidity.

Evidently, the network of the postal service, in combination with a government deposit guarantee, is better able to meet the needs of such savers than that of any other institution. Usually, the distribution of a commercial bank's branches in a country will match the distribution of its business clients. Network growth of normal banks is said to be business– or credit–led. In contrast, post offices are typically established where people live. Thus, the postal network is household – or savings–led. Post offices and postal agencies typically cover the country, both urban and rural areas, much more completely than the branch networks of banks.

But POSBs also exhibit serious weaknesses. One of them is that they channel funds away from the target groups and that they are not able to lend, at least as long as they are part of the postal system. In addition, POSBs in almost all countries are really the worst in terms of inefficiency one can find. Their success in mobilizing savings and the quality of service to customers is notoriously bad. Why is this so? The reason is the ill–conceived governance structure. It is the postal system which would have to do the work, and the Treasury would benefit from good work of the POSB. Quite naturally, the postal system lacks all genuine incentives to strive for a better performance in its banking operations as long as it sees no benefit for itself. In section 3 of chapter E we will return to this conflict and describe how it can be eliminated.

E

IINSTITUTION BUILDING

1. Overview

This chapter is devoted to methodological and pragmatic issues: What can be done, and what needs to be done, in order to improve the supply of financial services to the poorer segments of the population in developing countries – and, in the final analysis, to improve the social and economic position of these target-groups? More specifically, how can financial institutions be enabled and motivated to provide these financial services on a permant basis and how can this process of institution–building be planned and implemented?

There is a great deal that can be done. Firstly, action could be taken to influence the economy as a whole in one way or another, or, secondly, such actions could focus on the financial sector as a whole. Thirdly, action could be even more focussed on individual financial institutions or, as the case may be, on their customers. As in the preceding chapters, the term 'financial institution' is understood, in the broadest sense of the term, to include all actual and potential providers of financial services and the interaction with their customers.

Intervention at the level of the whole economy and at the level of the financial sector would be called "structural adjustment program" and "financial sector reform", respectively, if undertaken in a comprehensive and systematic way. Support to financial institutions is called "institution building".

Even though we are not concerned here with the normative and pragmatic issues of how to undertake or support structural adjustment and financial sector reform, it is important to take the financial sector and the general economy, particularly the need for reform at these levels, into account as "parameters" for institution building. It is for this reason, and only in terms of this aspect, that these parameters will be discussed in section 2 of this chapter.

But this study is devoted primarily to a discussion of what can be done at the level of the individual financial institution. The issues which are relevant for the individual institution are the subject of section 3. Our orientation, which calls for support, intervention or policy formulation at the level of the individual financial institution, is a reflection of our conviction that, from the standpoint of development policy, the marginal benefits of gearing efforts to institution building can be expected to be high if they are aimed at those types of institutions which have the capacity to reach large numbers of clients. Section 3.4 covers central issues of institution building on the donor side.

Figure 5 illustrates the relationships between the economy, the financial sector and financial institutions on the one hand, and between structural adjustment, financial sector reform and institution–building on the other. It shows that institution–building has to be regarded as an integral element of financial sector reform and, in fact, as a step towards general economic reform. Institution–building efforts that were undertaken without due regard for the wider context of the financial system and the conomy as a whole would most likely fail in the first place.

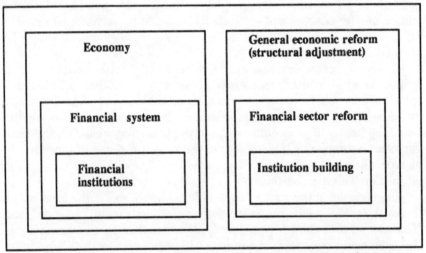

Figure 5:   *Economy, finance and institution–building: structure and reform*

2. The Relevant Parameters for Institution Building

2.1 The Scope and Nature of General Economic Reform and Financial Sector Reform

Even when it is the objective to design and implement a project geared to an individual financial institution, an evaluation of the financial system in its entirety and the state of the real economy, the monetary system and the legal, institutional and political parameters is indispensable. Is there a demand for the kind of financial services which the institution under consideration provides or might provide? What influence do monetary and fiscal policy have on the state of the economy and on the demand for credit and deposit facilities? Does the regulatory framework permit the institution to pursue a sound policy?

These are not easy questions to answer, even under stable conditions. And they become all the more problematic when reforms have begun to induce change in the relevant parameters. Therefore, a brief look at the nature and scope of these reforms is necessary at this point.

Although the situation varies considerably from one country to another, general economic reform ("structural adjustment") typically covers four areas.

(i) Macro-economic reform of the monetary, fiscal and exchange rate regimes and trade liberalization. The main problem involved here is which sequence of steps should be followed to achieve stabilization and liberalization.

(ii) Real-sector reform. The core issues are related to improving efficiency in industry, agriculture, commerce etc. through deregulation and competition.

(iii) Legal, institutional and political reform. The current trend is to reduce substantially the direct involvement of the state or the government in the economy, to make administrative processes more transparent and predictable, and to strengthen private property rights.

(iv) Financial sector reforms, as initiated and supported by the World Bank, the Inter-American Development Bank and major national donors, typically comprising the following five elements:

Rehabilitation of banks through financial and organizational measures. This tends to be a painful and lengthy process, as it requires that hidden portfolio problems be brought out into the open, that inefficient personnel be dismissed, that entire banks or bank branches be closed, that their capital base be restructured, etc.

- Deregulation and liberalization applying to the interest rates which a financial institution can pay and charge, the selection of sectors in which lending is permitted, and many other aspects of banking operations.
- Creation or strengthening of a bank supervisory institution.
- Limitation and even reduction of the discretionary powers óf the government deriving from its many roles as owner, regulator and major borrower–customer of the banking system.
- Lowering of entry and exit barriers into and out of the banking sector. It should become easier to establish new banks and close down others, as well as replace management teams in existing institutions, if advisable.

2.2 The Implications of General Economic and Financial Sector Reforms for Institution Building

In line with our focus on institution building at the level of the individual financial institution we only mention briefly some of the relationships which exist between the three non–financial elements of a general economic reform – monetary reform, real–sector reform and legal–institutional reform – and financial sector reform (#1 in Figure 6), between these elements and institution building (#2) and between financial sector reform and institution building (#3).

Non–financial reform and financial sector reform
Financial sector reform is an essential element of comprehensive economic reform, given the fact that the financial sector is crucial for economic growth and has, moreover, been in extremely poor shape in most developing countries for a long time.

Financial sector reform is rarely among the first steps taken in the implementation of a general economic reform or structural adjustment program. If monetary and fiscal reforms have not resulted in any appreciable degree of macroeconomic stabilization, interest rate deregulation would not be advisable. Yet, without interest rate deregulation, a reform of the financial sector is bound to lead to chaos (Diaz–Alejandro, 1985). Therefore, monetary and fiscal reform should precede financial sector reform.

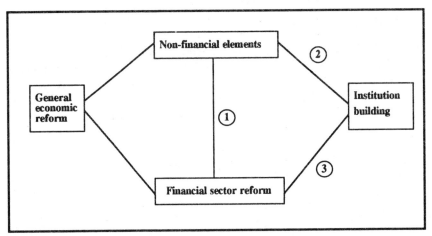

Figure 6:   *The different types of reform and their relationship*

More often than not, stabilization and liberalization are painful processes. They create problems for the borrowers and, as a consequence, for the financial institutions who lend to them. Or they bring out into the open problems, which had existed but were hidden, at the level of the borrowers and in the portfolios of the the financial institutions. These effects make a comprehensive financial sector reform not only more difficult, but also more important.

Non-financial elements of general economic reform and institution building

Among other things, the non-financial elements of a general economic reform tend to have the following implications for institution building:

The quality of the portfolios of those financial institutions which have a specific target-group orientation and are thus the focus of our concern here may also be adversely affected by the consequences of stabilization and liberalization. This is all the more likely to be the case in that those borrowers among the poor who are only able to build up a business because of existing distortions, overregulation, etc., are particularly vulnerable to the hazards of adjustment. For instance, the informal sector enterprises in the service and repair sectors typically suffer when restrictions on imports are eased, which is a central objective of structural adjustment policies.

Stabilization and structural adjustment often lead to massive lay-offs and a problem of "redeployment". This is a challenge, and probably a risky one, for development-oriented financial institutions, as they are often called upon to help the "redeployed" people to build up new businesses.

Monetary as well as institutional reform may have massive implications for what target–group–oriented financial institutions are permitted to do. Stability and a "reasonable" legal, institutional and political system are certainly helpful for institution–building efforts. However, it would be wrong to believe that macroeconomic reforms in this field are an indispensable prerequisite for target–group–oriented banking.

Financial sector reform and institution building

One should not expect that even an extremely far–reaching and successful financial sector reform would eliminate the need for specific efforts to initiate and support target–group–oriented financial institutions: There does not seem to be a "market mechanism" which would induce established financial institutions to start providing financial services to the lower–income target groups as soon as a financial sector reform has taken place. In the very long run, the competitive pressure on banks might have the desirable effect of making them less discriminatory. However, even in the medium– to long–term, they will have other strategic options, such as financing external trade, and experience indicates that they prefer these other options and are reluctant to serve the poorer segments of the population if they are not given specific incentives and technical assistance to motivate and enable them to address the "mass market" of the poor.

In fact, the opposite is true in many countries, especially in Africa: In several countries a financial sector reform under the auspices of the World Bank and other donors has led to the closing of all banks which would even consider lending to an informal–sector producer, for example. There were certainly good reasons for closing these banks, as they were insolvent, inefficient, corrupt, etc. However, the unintended consequence of the reformers' effort to stabilize the financial system as a whole was that the access to banking services was made extremely difficult for the target group.

A viable financial institution needs an adequate "constitution." For this, two things are almost invariably necessary: the presence of a powerful and professional supervisory authority for financial institutions, and strict limitations on the discretionary power of the government system to use and abuse the facilities of the financial institutions. Therefore, a well–functioning supervisory body and restrictive rules for the government are the two elements of financial sector reform which would be most conducive to institution building.

The rehabilitation of an existing bank which encounters serious financial difficulties in the course of financial sector reform offers an opportunity to change it fundamentally in such a way that it can become sustainable and target–group–oriented. This strategy of "building upon ruins" is particularly worth considering if the bank has a large branch network.

In many countries, entry into the formal financial sector, be it by founding a new institution or formalizing ("upgrading") an existing one, has been virtually impossible for an extended period of time. One element of financial sector reform is to lower the entry barriers. This can prove to be very important in the context of institution building.

Easy exit is equally important: Threatening to close down a financial institution if it loses too much money or to replace an incumbent management if it fails to perform properly must be one of the core elements of an incentive system designed to govern the conduct of a financial institution. A threat is only credible if it is real. It must be possible to close banks and replace managers without causing excessive damage to depositors. Financial sector reform must make closings and firings possible from a legal, institutional and economic standpoint.

These are just some of the many examples of the ways in which a financial sector reform can influence the task of institution building. Summing up, one can clearly state that financial sector reform is a step towards institution building. The converse of this statement is even more important: Institution building efforts at the level of the individual financial institution should always be such that they contribute to a reform of the financial sector as a whole. They should not pursue objectives which are at variance with the objectives of a financial sector reform; they should explore the possibilities for financial sector reform; they should help to create an awareness of the fact that financial sector reform may be called for; or, they might be aimed at alleviating the harsh consequences which a financial sector reform may have for the target population.

3. Institution Building Methodology

3.1   Approaches to Institution Building: a Critical Review

In the context of institution building and individual financial sector projects, development planners and administrators rightly stress the importance of having viable strategies and discuss the merits of finding innovative ways to provide financial services to target groups that have long been denied access to the formal financial system. For practical reasons, and specifically in the interest of facilitating planning and deci-sion-making as well as communication, a proper understanding of the available strategies would appear to be highly advisable.

3.1.1 The "Three-Strategies View": Upgrading, Downgrading, and Linking

Among experts of development aid working in the field of finance, a list of three so-called innovative strategies of institution building has gained prominence in recent years. The strategies making up this list are called upgrading, downgrading and linking. It seems that all interesting, innovative projects fall into one of these three categories. Moreover, they seem to be regarded as a set of mutually exclusive options, requiring planners in donor organizations and technical assistance units to make up their minds as to which of the three strategies they should adopt, either in the individual case or as a general policy decision.

What is the idea behind the standard list of three "innovative strategies"? Those who suggest that upgrading, downgrading and linking make up the selection of available strategies do so on the basis of what they feel is a realistic view of the situation in developing countries: There are two types of institutions worth considering for the provision of target-group-oriented services. The first type are institutions from the formal or informal sector which are not financial institutions in the legal sense, but are, or might be, involved in providing financial services. They typically are not linked to the government. In a broad sense of the term we call them "NGROs" in the present discussion. The acronym NGRO stands for "non government-related organization". The broad class of NGROs comprises NGOs (non-governmental organizations) and PVOs (private volunteer organizations) in the conventional definition[7], self-help groups and other informal-sector groups, donor-initiated rotating funds and credit programmes, cooperative-type organizations and many others. The generally held view is that, in terms of social and physical proximity, these "NGROs" typically are close to the target groups, they are socially motivated and development-oriented. At the same time, however, they typically are not very professional in their handling of financial business,

---

[7]   NGOs and PVOs are institutions like charitable foundations set up and run by people who do not themselves belong to the target groups. In the North-American context the two terms are not used synonymously; the term NGO refers to organizations in developing countries, like the Fundacion Dominicana de Desarollo (FDD), while the term PVO denotes similar organizations in donor countries, e.g. the industry sponsored Swiss foundation FUNDES.

and are also not well-connected to the financial system as a whole. Consequently, they also typically exhibit high costs and tend to be short-lived. Their potential to reach and serve target groups is their principal strength, while inefficiency, financial incompetence and short lifespans are their major weaknesses.

The other type of institution is that of banks or similar entities in the formal sector. Generally speaking, they are not close to the target groups in terms of social and physical proximity, nor would it be easy for them to reach the target groups even if they were so inclined. On the other hand, they at least have a reputation for being efficient and cost-conscious in what they do, and they are known for being relatively stable institutions which provide whatever services they do provide on a long-term basis.

It is from this plausible assessment of the state of affairs that the three strategies are, in turn, derived. Those who value the efficiency and presumed stability of banks highly advocate the *downgrading* strategy. It consists of a set of measures which would enable the banks to become more accessible and closer to the target groups of development policy. As an example, we would cite a well-established development bank in a specific country in Africa. In order to "downgrade" this bank, donors provided funding and support for a special small business financing department. Support took the form of providing specialized training for the personnel of this department and equipping them with their own computers. It even included the assistance of an advisor, whose orientation to social work was to be introduced at the bank. The advisor also tried to raise the level of awareness on the part of general management with respect to the importance and problems of target-group financing. Of course, there are various, specific measures which would contribute to downgrading in a given case.

Development planners who regard proximity to the target groups as the most important factor, while not losing sight of the limitations which are characteristic of NGROs may consider *upgrading* as an alternative. The term "upgrading" implies more than simply enlarging an institution or expanding the scope and improving the quality of its operations; rather, it contains an element of qualitative transformation. Efforts are undertaken to make a target-group-oriented institution more efficient, more stable and more professional. The advisor in charge would introduce elements of a banker's mentality at the NGRO. He or she should be an expert in credit extension, administration and controlling. In all likelihood, his or her task would be to press for a transformation of the NGRO into something more formal, even more bank-like. These efforts of becoming more formal, should of course, not suppress the virtues of target-group orientation. In the context of an upgrading strategy, it should be borne in mind that, not infrequently, the people who run and dominate an NGRO vigorously oppose its transformation. There are often personal reasons for this: life is easier and less complicated for an NGRO which is "soft" on credit, is friendly and grants favours, than it is for a bank which has to be "tough". Not infrequently the *de facto*-owners of an NGRO also find their present situation helpful when it comes to solliciting funds form donors. NGROs do have easier access to "soft" donor funds than banks have. Typically, however, the opposition to upgrading is presented vis-à-vis the public and in particular the donors by pointing out a concern over the risk of losing the target-group orientation instead of the true (and personal) motives.

Some experts (e.g. Seibel, 1989) may think that it is either impossible or too difficult to supplement the presumed strengths of a bank by introducing a social orientation, or, by the same token, that an NGRO would eventually forfeit its social orientation if it were made more formal. Therefore, they would advocate pursuing a third strategy, namely *linking*. Linking can take many forms. For example, a bank might cooperate with an established NGRO by providing the latter with funding for the NGO's own projects or for onlending. Or, the bank may use informal groups as distributors or collectors of funds, as guarantors, or as advisors in its credit-granting decisions.

3.1.2 A Critique of the "Three-Strategies View"

Most of the innovative projects in the field of financial institution building initiated in recent years fall into one of the three categories mentioned – upgrading, downgrading and linking. That is why development aid practitioners discuss these strategies, analyse when and where they are applicable and assess their respective merits and limitations. The approach that is presumably taken in deciding which strategy or combination of strategies to employ can be represented in the form of a decision tree (see Figure 7).

However, it would be grossly misleading to assume that these three strategies alone, taken individually or as a closed set of alternate or mutually exclusive options, provide the menu from which to choose a general policy for a donor or an executing agency. A view of this nature diverts the focus of attention and discussion away from the relevant aspects, and could even lead to unwise decisions. Because the trichotomy of upgrading, downgrading and linking clearly dominates current professional thinking, we find it justified to present a criticism of this approach at some length. There are three logical reasons why we object to the "three-strategies view".

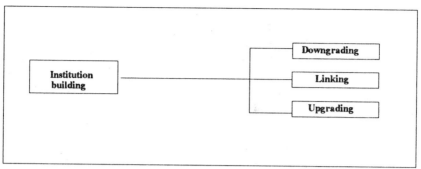

Figure 7:   *Selecting a strategy for institution building: the simple decision tree with three standard strategies*

1) Inconsistency: As is immediately clear from the above explanation, upgrading and downgrading cannot be regarded as alternatives with reference to one and the same institution. If "downgrading" were understood to mean "making more target–group–oriented", and "upgrading" as "making more professional and efficient", then these two options could, and should, be pursued simultaneously. Nor can downgrading and linking be regarded as alternatives. Rather, linking is one option, one specific measure, which is available in order to improve the target–group orientation.

2) Incompleteness: The list of available strategies is incomplete. Those who advocate a closed set of three strategies implicitly assume that the institution to be upgraded, downgraded or linked already exists. Yet, the creation of a new institution, or even a new type of institution, is certainly another option which is also available. The history of development finance abounds with attempts to create new institutions. If the option of creating a new institution is added, the decision tree looks like the one in Figure 8 on the next page.

It would seem that, in addition to the first three options and the option of building new institutions, there is also the possibility of restructuring institutions in the sense of initiating essential changes, as opposed to modifications. The three standard strategies are mere modifications of existing institutions (see Figure 9).

However, the distinction between "essential" and minor changes is not operational. Thus, the attempt to set the decision problem straight by including options that have been overlooked does not do much to clarify the situation.

86

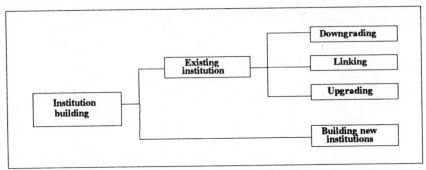

Figure 8: *Selecting a strategy for institution building: the enlarged decision tree*

3) Inappropriateness: Downgrading in the sense explained above, i.e. making an institution more target–group–oriented, is not a strategy at all. It is not a measure or a bundle of measures designed to attain an objective, but rather a suggestive term which describes the objective as such. The same would apply to "upgrading" if this term were taken to mean "making more professional or stable or efficient". "Upgrading" can only be considered a proper strategy if it is understood to mean making an institution more formal or more like a bank.

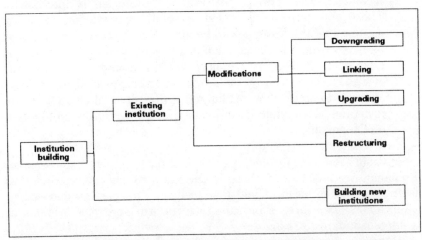

Figure 9: *Selecting a strategy for institution building: the complete decision tree*

These three points of logical criticism are intended to demonstrate that the standard list of "strategies" or an expanded version thereof cannot serve as a decision–making tool.

3.1.3 Project Design as a Decision Problem

When deciding how to improve a financial institution through a development aid project, the planners have to make their objectives – and, in fact, the hierarchy of relevant objectives – and their value judgements and factual assumptions explicit.

The ultimate and exclusive objective in the long run is to improve the social and economic situation of the target population. This needs to be made more specific in the framework of project planning: Any good project in the field of finance should contribute to shaping or influencing the financial sector of the developing country under consideration in such a way that there will be financial institutions which are, and remain, able and motivated to provide quality financial services with moderate operating and transaction costs to large segments of the population. At the level of the financial institution which is to be supported and improved, this objective corresponds to achieving the desired property of "target–group orientation".

Although target–group orientation is the only objective of institution building in the long run, planning efforts have to take the medium– and short–term perspective into account as well. In the medium term, target–group orientation is not the sole objective, because the prospects of a financial institution of being able to serve the target groups over the long term depend on two factors. One is the presence of a political, institutional and economic environment that is conducive to such an orientation; this factor has been touched on in section 2 above. The other factor concerns the policy and structure of the financial institution under consideration – with structure inevitably shaping policy in the medium– to long term: An institution which is fragile cannot pursue a target–group–oriented policy for long; nor can an institution which is financially so weak that it falls prey to those socio–economic groups which are not really concerned about the poorer people. Therefore, on the operational level and over the medium–term, which is the normal planning horizon of development bureaucrats, sustainability is an equally important objective: A target–group oriented institution has to be professional, financially and organisationally stable and efficient in order to be permanently able to serve the target groups.

Unprofessional, unstable and inefficient institutions are undesirable even if their short–term target–group orientation is extremely strong, because, in the final analysis, they prove to be too costly, and they do not take poor people seriously. They create expectations which they cannot fulfill, and introduce an additional element of instability into the lives of people who are truly in need of stability and some degree of reliability for the future. Thus, in the medium term, target–group orientation and sustainability are equally important objectives. In the short run, institutional sustainability may even appear to be the more important of the two. Technically speaking, target–group–orientation is the objective which is to be maximized subject to the strict constraint of sustainability.

With these two desiderata or objectives in mind, planners must tackle three issues in the framework of their project for support and intervention geared to a financial institution: The first issue is how the two objectives should be weighted in a development aid project.

The second issue concerns the "substance" of the support: What steps should be taken by the supporting organisation, be it a donor or an executing agency, to achieve the project aims? This may involve the provision of advisors, for example, or training measures or data processing equipment. Depending on the specific situation, the instruments of support have to be tailored to suit the specific project aims. For example, an advisor could be commissioned to strengthen the target–group orientation and help to establish linkages between a bank and self–help groups. Alternatively, the advisor could have the task of making an institution from the broadly defined group of NGROs more professional and more efficient, and help to transform it into a "real" financial institution ("upgrading", narrowly defined).

For a long time, the issue of "substance" – i.e. what kind of support – has been discussed in terms of the alternatives of financial versus technical cooperation (see chapter B). Financial support in the form of subsidized loans to the financial institution(s) under consideration has been regarded as the more important form of support, with technical cooperation mainly serving the purpose of ensuring that the funds are channeled to the intended beneficiaries. More recently, technical assistance for institution building has gained more recognition as an approach in its own right. In some cases, technical assistance projects are now supported by a component of financial assistance which may take the form of a grant or a loan. There is no point in denying that provision of funds as grants or loans on favourable terms often has to be a component of a "package" which contains technical assistance for institution building as the main component. There may be several reasons for adding the financial component to the package. One is that there is simply a demand for loanable funds which cannot be satisfied in other ways. A second reason may derive from the bargaining power of recipient institutions in developing country vis-à-vis the donors from industrial countries: Some financial institutions are such attractive partners for donors that they can request a price for permitting the donors to work with them and allowing them to pursue their development goals through this collaboration. The financial assistance, and in particular its grant component, is the price. Or, in other words, some partners in developing countries have to be "bribed" through a financial contribution in order to make them accept the technical cooperation. Note that there is nothing wrong with, or morally objectionable about, such "deals". Finally, there may be reasons stemming from the donor side: Several important donor institutions are themselves under pressure to make sizable amounts of money flow to the developing world, and they tend to talk recipients into requesting and "absorbing" a credit or grant component. This is particularly true in the case of donor institutions which are themselves banks and/or are forced to use up budgeted funds.

The serious drawbacks of "financial cooperation" are well known (Von Pischke, Adams, Donald, 1984; and in particular Vogel, 1986). Still, the first two reasons may make sense in some cases. But we think donors should restrict themselves as much as possible to providing technical assistance for institution building.

The third issue concerns the intensity of a development project's interference or intervention in an institution or, as the case may be, in the financial system of the partner country. The spectrum ranges from a minimum of interference or modification to far-reaching measures to restructure and build new institutions. Typically the intensity of inter-vention depends on the "substance" of the support and on the objective.

Obviously, the project design which is advisable in a given situation can, and should, differ from case to case in terms of the three dimensions: (1) project aim, (2) substance or types of support, and (3) intensity of intervention. Even so, is a general trend discernible which favours one or the other and other project design? First of all, the role of financial cooperation or lending to financial institutions in developing countries seems, hopefully, to lose ground to technical cooperation and institution building. But this trend is not yet strong. There also seems to be some change under way in the narrower field of institution building proper: From the literature and our discussions with experts in many donor organisations, we have gained the impression that there is still a preference for projects which combine an emphasis on direct target-group orientation with low intensity of intervention ("subsidiarity principle") and e.g. training measures. However, there is a small but growing number of experts who think that, in the long-term interest of those who need development aid most, an increasing focus on the objective of sustainability combined with a high intensity of intervention is necessary and justified. We count ourselves among those in the second group. In the remainder of this chapter we discuss specific measures which can be undertaken to better achieve the objectives of target-group orientation and sustainability.

3.2   Enhancing Target–Group Orientation

3.2.1   General Remarks

In this study we consider an institution to be target–group–oriented if it provides the kind of financial services which the target groups demand in an accessible and adequate way and at reasonable cost.

Openness vis-à--vis the target groups of the poor (in a broad sense) and concern for their social and economic welfare are an indispensable requirement for a financial institution in the formal, semi–formal or informal sector to be eligible as a partner for cooperation. This necessarily raises the question of what such an institution can do to become more target–group–oriented than it used to be, or more so than other institutions in the respective country. And what steps could be taken by development bureaucrats in donor organisations and executing agencies to motivate or pressure an institution to become more target–group–oriented? Unfortunately, there is no list of recipes or pat solutions which would be applicable everywhere in more or less the same way. Be that as it may, there are a number of general principles – and lessons learned from experience – which we want to share with the reader, who can apply them as required in specific cases, before we proceed to discuss the subject in detail.

First of all, target–group orientation is more a matter of an institution's general policy or "corporate culture" than of the clever application of techniques or "tricks of the trade". There is ample empirical evidence to support this assessment, given the pervasive failure of attempts to add a small–scale or informal–sector (microenterprise) department to an institution which is generally oriented towards established customers in the modern sector (see e.g. Levitsky, 1986) and which does not have a genuine incentive to develop an orientation towards poorer target groups. There can be no doubt that this has happened; however, one can now question the relevance of this experience as a justification for pessimistic predictions of a general nature since all of the earlier attempts – and failures – were undertaken in an unfavourable environment, and with an inadequate method of "light" intervention. When interest rates are clearly negative in real terms, granting a loan is a gift and a favour to the borrower. Even several well–meaning and technically competent advisors attached to a small–scale department would certainly not be able to talk the bank management into giving away this gift to a target group to which they have never had any close ties. Now, after financial repression has been largely eliminated in many countries, banks have to find profitable application for their funds, and thus they may be much more open to accept changes in their policies and even in their "corporate culture".

Secondly, a lasting target–group orientation towards the poorer population is often not in the interest of those who have an influence on the general policy of the institution; we shall return to this point later on.

Thirdly, target–group orientation does not consist in trying to make the customers do what "benevolent" development planners would like them to do, nor of a paternalistic attitude of knowing what the target groups "really need" better than they themselves do. Rather, it involves the willingness to listen, look and learn about the needs – and the demand – for financial services among the target groups, and it involves the ability and the willingness (prompted by financial pressure) to do so.

Finally, target–group–oriented banking for and with the poor should not be regarded primarily as social work, but as a very serious business (Jackelen, 1989) requiring cost coverage. In fact, the often used term "financial service" tends to obscure the conflict which exists between the philosophies of social service which is – for good reasons – not regarded and rendered in a business–like way on the one side, and banking in the narrow sense of the word of strict business.

3.2.2 The Supply of Relevant Financial Services to the Target Groups in a Marketing Perspective

What kinds of products should a target–group oriented financial institution provide? What characteristics should the products have? How should they be distributed and priced? How should the institution provide information to its customers? These are standard marketing issues which have proved to be helpful in thinking about development projects as well (Kotler/Roberto, 1989). Despite our general disclaimer that there is no cookbook approach, a few general statements can be made in answering some of these questions. We organize these statements in accordance with a standard marketing classification.

Products:

Customers of financial institutions everywhere in the world require and demand a broad spectrum of financial services which include

- deposit or savings facilities
- credit or borrowing facilities
- payment or money transfer services
- risk–management and insurance services.

All of these services can take different forms; for instance, the demand for credit may vary according to purpose or use, term to maturity and risk characteristics. Although one cannot say in general terms what products are demanded by the target groups among the poorer population, by now it is a generally accepted view that many members of the target groups demand additional kinds of services, namely deposit services, payment transfers and others, and not merely the provision of credit for productive purposes. Yet, production–oriented credit is the only service which some formal–sector development finance institutions, as well as most special, donor–funded programmes and NGROs have provided to date. Even credit does not necessarily have to be extended in the form of a loan; not infrequently, people need liquidity and thus access to an overdraft facility or a line of credit more than they need an actual loan. Only very few institutions which believe themselves to be target–group–oriented provide lines of credit (even if their customers are traders) or sufficiently liquid deposit facilities.

Empirical investigations in (rural) Africa have consistently shown that the typical household demands most of all deposit facilities which afford protection against theft, inflation, family pressures and the saver's own impatience or sudden impulse to spend money. It is well–known that in Africa the money collectors and keepers in the informal financial sector are paid for providing such services (Bentil *et al.*, 1988).

Product design.

The product design has to be geared to the attributes of the services provided. If credit services are involved, attributes such as speed of processing and disbursement, paperwork, term to maturity, flexibility, security or collateral requirements, strictness in enforcing repayment, etc., come to mind. In the case of deposits, convenience of withdrawal and liquidity, the institution's treatment of depositors, and the interest on deposits, are important aspects of product design.

Many of the factors involved in product design are case–specific for two reasons: firstly, different customers may assign different values to certain product characteristics, such as collateral requirements for a loan; and, secondly, whereas in some cases financial institutions are in a position to make a product more attractive by adding a particular feature such as liquidity of savings deposits, this may not be feasible in other cases. It would be naive to call a financial institution target–group–oriented if, and only if, it does not require the provision of security for loans or if it permits unlimited withdrawals of deposits at all times. Instead we would require that a target–group–oriented financial institution try to learn as much as it can about the customers' demands and problems and make a genuine effort to design its products as well as it can in order to meet these demands without jeopardizing its own sustainability. Security requirements serve as one example: Conventional forms of credit security such as land titles are often not available to the target group; a bad bank, however, would nevertheless make the loan conditional on the provision of such securities. Yet, a bank could accept other forms of collateral such as pledges or group guarantees. Or it could relax security requirements and instead design its credit policy in such a way that borrowers are willing to repay in order to protect their reputations and thus preserve their access to credit (Schmidt/Kropp, 1987, pp. 57-67). A good, target-group–oriented bank would carefully weigh these alternatives and select the one which is easiest for its customers to bear.

With respect to deposit facilities as well, the issue is not one of simply identifying the optimal product characteristics irrespective of their costs to the bank, but of arriving at an optimal design which takes into account the interests on both sides. In the practice of development finance, the question of product design is very rarely posed in this way. Instead, products are designed according to traditional practices or preconceived notions about the target groups and their social and economic characteristics and their presumed needs. For instance, group guarantees, or lending groups, are sometimes employed as a means of securing credit only because donors are so fond of seeing the members of target groups practice "solidarity".

We believe that judicious product design can greatly enhance the value of financial services to the designated target groups.

Much the same considerations as those involved in product design apply to the forms and channels of *distribution* for the products.

Pricing policy:

What prices can and should target–group–oriented financial institutions charge for their services? It has been traditionally held that the poor are unable to support market rates of interest and should there-fore be granted loans at subsidized rates. Is the charging of low interest rates an indication of a strong target–group orientation, and should financial institutions be encouraged to charge lower–than–market rates for the sake of an improved target-group orientation? The answer is: definitely not!

Subsidies have several negative consequences. Lower–than–market interest rates attract rent seekers. The excess demand results in rationing, and this typically favours those who are not from the target groups (Gonzalez–Vega, 1984). In fact, the opposite approach would be even better: Target-group–oriented financial institutions should charge higher interest rates than the "normal" banks to discourage borrowers who have no problems obtaining credit from the banks; this would enable them to reserve the scarce loanable funds for their target group.

Moreover, it is wrong to believe that the lending rate is very important for borrowers from poor target groups. What matters for them is access to credit, not subsidies. Access to "formal" credit is normally difficult for them, and their relevant alternatives are the money-lender or other informal sources which are usually much more expensive anyway.

In addition, almost all borrowing customers of target-group-oriented financial institutions do not seek loans for investing in long-term projects. Their demand for credit is mostly for short-terms only, and arises on short notice. Therefore, their credit demand is not at all interest-elastic, as the high interest rates which are accepted in the informal sector clearly show.

The basic reason for the irrelevance, or indeed counterproductive effect, of subsidizing interest rates is this: Borrowers do not, or should not, base their borrowing decisions on interest considerations alone. Rather, they base their calculations on total borrowing costs, part of which is accounted for by transaction costs, which include the value of waiting time, bribes, etc. In the case of one African country, a group of researchers has estimated that the transaction costs for an average loan to an average borrower are much higher than interest costs (Bentil *et al.,* 1988). Interest costs and transaction costs are normally negatively correlated. Higher interest costs tend to reduce e.g. waiting time and in some cases the need to pay bribes to the bank personnel because costumers who can obtain credit at lower costs from established banks would not stand in line trying to obtain loans from the target-group-oriented institution. Consequently, by raising interest costs, a target-group-oriented bank may, in the final analysis, even reduce total borrowing costs.

The distinction between total borrowing costs on the one side and its components of interest costs (including fees) and transaction costs on the other side is also important in the following respect: A high share of interest costs in total borrowing costs is preferable from the standpoint of the target groups because it produces a higher revenue for "their" financial institution and thus contributes to assuring the long-term availability of the services it supplies.

Advertising, communication and public relations.

An institution has to make known to its potential customers what services they can expect to receive from the institution. This calls for some form of advertising. It should also be made very clear that loans are not gifts: they are meant to be repaid! This is after all a matter for communications and public relations. In advertising and PR it is, in our opinion, absolutely necessary to be honest and treat the customers fairly. For instance, information which advertises contractual instead of effective borrowing rates should be avoided, as this is often grossly misleading[8]. Moreover, in a country characterized by financial repression, it is equally objectionable to advertise deposit facilities by pointing to the prospect of accumulating financial wealth: That is not why customers should save in a bank, given the fact that financial assets are continually losing value. If they put their savings in a bank, they (rightly) do so for other reasons.

In concluding this section, we can summarize as follows: A target-group–oriented financial institution should provide other services, in other forms and at different prices, than those which a "normal" bank would offer. Target–group orientation is a meaningful, operational concept for banking activity at the interface between bank and customer. Of course, there are limits on the extent to which financial services can be made available to meet all demands and to suit everyone's preferences. These limits are necessary and inevitable if the financial institution is to remain viable over the long term. Nevertheless, most financial institutions in developing countries do not seem to operate "at the frontier" (Von Pischke, 1991), which economists call the "efficiency frontier". They could manage to be both more target–group oriented and more sustainable.

3.3   Enhancing Sustainability

3.3.1   The Importance and Meaning of Sustainability

From the standpoint of development aid, it does not make much sense to work with institutions which are unstable, unprofessional and inefficient. Even if they are able to operate in a decidedly target–group–oriented manner for a short while, their overall development impact will almost invariably be negative: The unit costs of their services will prove to be extremely high, not only for the donor countries but also – if measured in terms of opportunity costs – for the developing countries. Moreover, a short burst of fireworks of target–group–relevant activity on the part of an institution which soon breaks down under the heavy load of its commitments may foster an unhealthy attitude towards development-

---

[8]   Confusion resulting from misleading information about interest rates for loans is particularly serious - and quite frequent - in the case of consumer loans which are repaid in regular monthly installments. Some banks advertise that they grant loans with "attractive", low interest rates. But these are contractual rates on the initial balance. They disregard that the outstanding balance declines over time so that the effective interest rate goes up to levels which make money lenders appear like welfare institutions.

oriented financial institutions. Poor people will learn that it is foolish to repay a loan, and they will be hesitant to deposit their savings in such institutions.

There are, of course, many good reasons for giving subsidies, gifts, etc. to poor people, but these welfare activities should always be clearly separated from any activity which even comes close to being "banking business". Not only the target groups but also those who run target-group-oriented institutions must learn that banking is "tough". It cannot be done otherwise.

Any institution which provides financial services must be structured and run in such a way that it can survive on its own. Why is the requirement that a target-group-oriented financial institution can cover its costs so extremely important? One part of the answer to this question has to do with considerations of allocational efficiency: Socially wasteful investment projects are not likely to be profitable for the investor. Financing such ventures is also not likely to be profitable for a financial institution. In this respect the requirement of cost coverage helps to avoid extremely (socially) inefficient investment decisions. However, in a distorted economy with a fragmented financial system, where external effects are common, this consideration does not apply at the margin: There may be projects which have a positive value for society but are negative for the investor and the financing institution, and vice versa. Cost coverage is, therefore, neither a necessary nor a sufficient condition for an efficient allocation of capital.

Consequently, the argument of allocational efficiency alone is not enough to justify the strict requirement that a financial institution must cover its costs. But there are also other arguments based on considerations of a political economy type: Heavy losses force an institution to seek financial support from powerful people. The support may be forthcoming as requested, but experience shows that it is obtained at a high price: in return for providing assistance, the helpful person, who in many cases is a politician, or a political institution will demand to have a say in the institution's lending decisions. This kind of influence tends to undermine the financial institution and diverts its attention away from its target group (Von Pischke *et al.*, 1981).

If a financial institution wants to cover its costs, it has to be realistic in measuring these costs. How can the relevant costs be defined and measured? Administrative costs and due provisions for non-repayment of loans are cost components which do not pose any conceptual problems, although there may be some practical problems of measurement. The situation may be different with regard to the costs of financing, especially the cost of equity under inflationary conditions.

The first question is: What are the characteristics of the "equity" of a development finance institution which is strongly supported by external donors? Equity in the economic sense is equity capital in the legal sense *plus* funds which have been given to the institution for onlending as a grant. Although the funds are donated and thus without payment obligation to the donor (who may be local or foreign), such equity should not be regarded as cost-free, because this would lead to faulty decisions: In an inflationary environment, treating donated funds as cost-free leads to decapitalisation, i.e. to a decrease in the real value, or purchasing power, of the equity funds available for lending to the target groups. Inflation can cause a financing institution to dwindle away, while it is working hard and successfully to be profitable in nominal terms. Therefore, out of pragmatic considerations, we suggest that at least the inflation rate be used as the cost of equity. If these costs are covered, it can be assumed that the lending power of equity will be maintained. If not even the equity is kept intact in real terms then there is serious reason for concern. A definition of the cost of equity which flashes an alarm signal in the case of a loss in real terms can help to protect the institution.

The definition of the cost of equity capital as the inflation rate has an important implication: Under inflationary conditions, equity, including donated funds for onlending, is often more costly than deposits and borrowed funds.

Requiring a lending institution to cover its costs may result in high prices for its services. As we have explained above, high prices for financial services should normally not pose a problem for target-group customers as far as lending is concerned. However, it would be a problem for the financial institution if there were no demand for its financial services when they are priced at cost covering rates: then the special, target-group oriented financial institution would not have any role to play. Due to a worldwide trend towards deregulation, there is now an increasing number of countries in which this seems to be the case and in which the existing formal and informal financial system is apparently adequate to meet the demand of the target population.

For some institutions, it seems to be a far too ambitious aim to cover all costs, including the cost of inflation. Even in nominal terms, profitability is often very difficult to achieve owing to the costs and risks of lending to economically unstable target groups and the nature of the administrative costs involved: There are at least some economies of scale in banking operations, as a considerable share of the administrative costs are fixed costs. In order to be able to spread them over a larger volume of business, target-group-oriented financial institutions are often forced to grow quickly during the first few years of their existence, and they must find ways to do so without incurring unbearable credit risks.

There are two reqirements which have to be met in order to ensure sustainability and survival of an institution and permanence of its role for the target group. Although they are in fact interrelated, they can be discussed separately here since they differ in terms of the underlying time perspective. The profitability requirement applies to the short– and medium–term perspective. Measures to enhance profitability are therefore short– and medium–term measures. The incentive requirement is based on a structural and medium–to long–term perspective. The two requirements are dicussed in the following two subsections.

3.3.2 The Profitability Requirement

Profitability is an accounting concept which attempts to measure income and sustainability. In the case of a financial institution (or bank), the profitability requirement can most easily be explained – and taken care of in the planning process – in terms of bank margins. A bank (or other financial institution) is profitable if, and only if, the gross margin of revenue minus financing costs is sufficient to cover administrative costs and risk–related costs.

This definition will be illustrated using the example of a hypothetical Bank B in country C. The balance sheet of Bank B contains four asset and four liability/capital items. Each of the assets has a realized gross return (in per cent per year) and accounts for a given share of total liabilities at any point in time. Note that equity "costs" (at least) as much as the inflation rate of country C, which we assume to be 20%.

Some of the rates of return and costs may be determined exogenously by relevant authorities, others appear to be market determined, and some are the result of decisions made in and by the bank. The same applies to the individual items in the total of assets and liabilites.

Judged by the standards used in industrial countries, this bank would appear to be a gold mine, as it has a gross margin of 9.4 per cent and a 10 per cent equity ratio. Also from a development standpoint it looks great as half of its loans are "small", which we assume to mean target–group–oriented, and it is able to mobilize all of the funds it lends to its customers. Let us assume that, in addition to interest income, Bank B has fee income amounting to 1 per cent of total assets, which de facto boosts the gross margin to 10.4 per cent.

However, the gross margin calculated on the basis of contractual interest payments – as it is done in the example – is only one determinant of profitability. The others are administrative costs, which can also be expressed as a "required" (or "cost–covering") margin, and loss rates on outstanding loans. Let us assume that, in the case of Bank B,

assets				liabilities/capital			
(1)	(2)	(3)	(4)	(1)	(2)	(3)	(4)
Item	share	return	(2) x (3)	Item	share	cost	(2) x (3)
cash	10%	0	0%	current deposits	30%	3%	9%
gov. securities	10%	15%	1.5%	fixed deposits	30%	14%	4.2%
"large" loans	40%	20%	8%	savings deposits	30%	10%	3%
"small" loans	40%	25%	10%	equity	10%	20%	2%
total assets	100%		19.5%	total liabilities	100%		10.1%

Table 4:   Balance sheet and basic profitability calculation for a
hypothetical bank

administrative costs are 8% of total assets/liabilities, and the loan loss rate
is 5% of all outstanding loans or 4% of total assets/liabilities. Given these
figures, which may in many cases be difficult to determine exactly, Bank
B is not profitable, and if the current situation were to prevail it would not
be able to survive without external support.

The crucial relation is

(interest + fee income) margin $\leqq$ admin. cost (margin) + loan loss rate.

In the above example, Bank B is not breaking even, as

9.4 %   +   1 %   <   8%   +   4 %

This way of characterizing the profitability requirement provides a
first indication of the range of measures which can be considered and
taken to improve profitability.

The first group of measures is related to the interest margin which is
determined by

1) the rates of return on asset classes and thus the bank's pricing policy or, in some cases, the external constraints relating to asset returns and pricing. In many cases it would seem feasible to increase contractual interest rates on loans. This is particularly true of small, target-group oriented loans as the demand exhibited by poor borrowers is typically not interest elastic (see section 3.3.1 above);

2) the composition of assets. Subject to liquidity requirements and relevant regulation, a bank can try to shift funds to more profitable asset classes. In the example used here it would appear that granting small loans is the most profitable use for funds. However, as we will see later, this is too good to be true. In general, small loans are not likely to be the most profitable asset class. Note that in these cases it would not be advisable to minimize the weight of this asset class as it is the objective of the bank, from a development perspective, to grant such loans;

3) the cost of the liability items. In order to maximize its profitability, a bank should try to pay as little as it can to depositors or other lenders. But here again, a development- or target-group related considerations limit the feasibility of such a policy, as paying "too low" interest rates on deposits from the poorer target-groups means providing a poorer-quality service to them in the field of deposit business. In addition, the supply of deposits seems to be much more interest elastic than the demand for credit;

4) the composition of liabilities. Since current and fixed deposits are likely to come from customers who are not the target groups in the development sense, a bank can try to reduce its average cost of capital by a policy of attracting the cheapest funds, which in many cases are current deposits. In some cases it may also be feasible to borrow funds from other institutions in order to reduce costs.

All of these options are subject to one very important qualification:

Not only regulations, market considerations and development considerations limit the scope for increasing returns and reducing costs of individual balance-sheet items, and for restructuring assets and liablities. Most of the changes discussed above will also have consequences in terms of adminstrative costs and loan losses, and these consequences have to be taken into account.

The second determinant of profitability refers to administrative costs and operational efficiency. Banks in developing countries typically do not operate very efficiently, and this is even more true of the credit-granting institutions which are not banks in the legal sense, which operate in developing countries and exhibit a certain degree of target–group orientation.

Banking, and in particular target–group oriented banking, is difficult and requires substaintial inputs of high–quality manpower and data processing, both of which are expensive. The productivity of banking services depends to a great degree on the type and level of training and on the organisation of administrative procedures and decision–making processes. In our consulting experience it has always been surprising how much administrative costs differ between institutions whose business activities are rather similar and which have similar balance sheet structures. This would indicate that in most individual cases there is considerable scope for cost reduction or for reducing administrative costs.

However, three general observations on administrative costs should be added: First, there is clearly a "learning curve" in target–group lending; unit costs decline over time in a sound institution. Second, there are at least some economies of scale; this implies that there may be a minimum size below which a target–group oriented institution is certainly inefficient. Third, and most important in our view, is the observation that cost–effectiveness depends very much on the corporate constitution and the incentives of the institution under consideration: No institution will operate efficiently if there is no strong pressure to do so, and a motive to adapt to this pressure.

The third determinant of profitability and the third group of measures refer to lending and loan losses as a cost factor ("risk costs"). Most financial institutions and special credit programmes serving poor target groups have collapsed in the past under the burden of heavy loan losses. This need not happen, however. If one takes a look at individual cases, one can almost always find specific mistakes in the design or implementation of credit programmes and institutions – mistakes which are probably also the reason why loan losses occurred in the first place. The following are among the most important mistakes in such cases:

- Lending is not based on demonstrated demand, but rather on the presumed need of borrowers.
- Lending is not based on a serious evaluation of the borrower and his/her ability to repay.
- Lending decisions are based on "most–likely estimates" and disregard the borrowers' business risk (Von Pischke, 1988).
- Lending is not practiced with a visible and credible determination to insist on repayment.
- Lending policy is not clear or consistent in design. Criteria are either not established or they are applied inconsistently.

- Collection efforts are insufficient.
- Diversification is insufficient.
- Even easily available forms of credit security are either not required or are not seized in the event of default.
- Loan sizes, terms to maturity and repayment patterns are not in line with borrowers' investment opportunities and income patterns.
- Loans are granted to friends, relatives and influential people who will not be pressed to repay.

Even if all of these mistakes are avoided, lending is still risky for the lender. The ability and willingness of a borrower to repay is never certain. However, there are techniques that can reduce the risk of default, such as

- careful credit evaluation,
- transparent arrangements governing repayment and interest payments,
- cautious determination of loan sizes,
- short terms to maturity,
- acceptance of various forms of credit security, such as group loans and group guarantees,
- personalizing the bank–customer relationship and invoking the borrower's pride as a motive for repayment,
- sequencing loans so that larger loans are obtainable on more favourable conditions after outstanding loans have been duly repaid.

The introduction of well–conceived credit–extension and collateral policies can go a long way towards reducing default rates. Most often, it is not so much a problem of devising the appropriate scheme, but rather of sticking to it despite adverse pressures, including the lender's own feeling that it is unfair to insist on repayment. Recent experience in poverty-oriented lending schemes indicates that it should be possible to lower loan loss rates to less than five percent. Such a low loss rate could then be compensated via the interest rate without increasing the probability of loan losses due to the mere fact that the interest rate is "too high".

The three determinants of profitability are of course interrelated. Administrative costs and expected loan losses increase with the share of loans in total assets, and may vary with the distribution between "small" and "large" loans.

While smaller loans are inevitably more costly to administer than larger loans, the relative risk costs cannot be assessed in general terms. In countries, in which political interference in the affairs of institutions is likely, larger loans tend to be more risky because a bank might be prevented from enforcing repayment.

The composition of the liability or deposit side also has some influence on administrative costs. Current deposits are cheap in terms of interest, but costly in terms of administration. These relationships are the reason why the calculation of profitability based on gross margin, administrative costs and risks alone, which was demonstrated at the beginning of this section (Table 4), is not enough to assess the potential of a bank to become viable, and is also not enough to provide a basis for sound planning. For these purposes it is necessary to divide the total administrative costs up into different parts and to allocate some parts as "variable costs" to specific balance sheet items. One would want to allocate these costs in such a way that increasing or decreasing the individual item would increase or decrease administrative costs correspondingly. In order to simplify matters – but not in such a way that the essential accuracy of data is impaired – , one could assume proportionality or linear cost functions. The cost sensivity factors are, of course, specific to individual institutions.

After all variable costs have thus been allocated, the remainder of the administrative costs is, by definition, fixed. In our example of Bank B with total administrative costs of 8 per cent of total assets and liabilities, we assume that 6.5 per cent can be allocated as is shown in Table 5. From column (6), 5.3 per cent are "caused" by the lending business, and can thus be allocated to the loans, and 1.2 per cent are generated by the deposit business. 1.5 per cent are fixed costs. Expected loss rates can be allocated as "risk costs" to the lending business in a similar way. After reducing gross rates of return by allocated administrative costs and expected loss rates, and, correspondingly, increasing capital costs by administrative costs, one arrives at adjusted rates of return and adjusted financing costs. They indicate how a variation in the share of each item in the balance sheet would affect the profitability of the bank.

Table 5 shows that Bank B in our example is incurring losses from its operations which amount to 1.1 per cent of total assets/liabilities (column 10). So there is no contribution to the coverage of the fixed administrative costs of 1.5 per cent. If table 5 showed the situation of a real bank in a developing country, Bank B would clearly stand out as a successful bank because it has a current deficit of only 2.6 per cent. It would appear that either by modifying the facts which underly the individual entries in Table 5, i.e. by increasing returns and cutting costs, or by varying the structure of assets and liabilities, this bank would be in a position to achieve cost-coverage. If it could at least achieve a situation in which average net returns exceeded average total cost of funds, there would be the additional option of growth leading to a relative reduction of the fixed administrative costs.

(1)	(2)	(3)	(4)	(5)	(6)	(7)	(8)	(9)	(10)
I. ASSETS	share in total assets	gross return	(2)x(3)	admin. costs	(2)x(5)	risk-costs	(2)x(7)	net return	(2)x(9)
cash	10%	--	--	--	--	--	--	0	
gov.securities	10%	15%	1.5%	1%	0.1%	--	--	14%	1.4%
"large" loans	40%	20%	8%	3%	1.2%	5%	2%	12%	4.8%
"small" loans	40%	25%	10%	10%	4%	5%	2%	10%	4%
total assets	100%		19.5%		5.3%		4%		10.2%
II. LIABILITIES/ CAPITAL	share in total liab.	net costs	(2)x(3)	admin. costs.	(2)x(5)	--	--	full costs	(2)x(9)
curr. deposits	30%	3%	0.9%	3%	0.9%	--	--	6%	1.8%
fixed deposits	30%	14%	4.2%	0	0	--	--	14%	4.2%
savings deposits	30%	10%	3%	1%	0.3%	--	--	11%	3.3%
equity	10%	20%	2%	--	--	--	--	20%	2%
total liabilities	100%		10.1%		1.2%				11.3%

<u>Table 5</u>: *Balance sheet and cost allocation for a hypothetical bank*

How high is the interest margin which a target group–oriented institution must earn in order to cover its costs? Of course it depends on many factors, including productivity – e.g. the number of clients taken care of by one loan officer – and the kind of services which are being provided.

As a rough–and–ready estimate of the required margin of a target–group–oriented financial institution operating in a difficult environment, the following figures may provide some orientation: A gross margin of 10 per cent should be enough to cover administrative costs of some 5 per cent and loan losses of about the same size. It is, in our view, possible to achieve such margins and cost ratios through good project design and careful implementation and management.

All these considerations lead us to believe that it is possible to provide financial services, mainly deposit services and some forms of credit, to the poorer target population without incurring the need for permanent subsidies to an institution which provides such services. Of course, it is not an easy task to combine target–group orientation and cost coverage, but there are now at least some positive examples which demonstrate that it can be done.

3.3.3 The Incentive Requirement

This leads us to the fourth group of measures aimed at stabilizing target group–oriented institutions. They refer to the design of an adequate and sound constitution. The term "constitution" (or, alternatively, governance structure) signifies the distribution of powers among those who can influence the policy decisions of the institution, the limitations to such powers and the incentives to use the powers. The problem involved in the design constitution is this: How can powers be distributed and restricted, and how can incentives be set in such a way that the behaviour of the relevant individuals in their respective roles leads to a "behaviour" on the part of the institution which is geared to both target–group orientation and survival of the organization (Fama/Jensen, 1983)?

A suitable constitution clarifies the rights and responsibilities of at least four groups of actors: the management, the owners, a group of external monitors and the legal constraints which they impose and enforce, and the customers or target groups. Before discussing the details, it is necessary to point out the main structural threats to the stability, and even the survival, of a potentially target–group–oriented financial institution. They are all manifestations of incentive problems, or, more precisely, of a lack of properly adjusted incentives.

- Borrowers are quite naturally a threat to the stability of such an institution because they will always seek to avoid repayment.
- A lazy, self-serving or incompetent management may be unwilling or unable to pursue a prudent and efficient policy.
- Anyone who is in a position to act like an owner and determine the institution's general policy may try to influence it in such a way that the orientation towards poorer target groups is lost.
- Regulators or bank supervisors may have no authority or only inadequate instruments, or may simply lack the motivation, to avoid the accumulation of deficits.
- Politicians in whatever role may try to gain influence and use the institution as an instrument to distribute "favours" to their followers and electorate.
- Anyone in a relevant position may threaten the institution's survival by creating unrealistic expectations about the extent to which it can afford to be more socially receptive.

Everyone tends to regard a financial institution and, to a greater degree, a special credit programme or even a "revolving fund", as a pile of money that is "up for grabs". This way of looking at things is utterly realistic! Some want the money to enrich themselves, improve their political position or make their lives more comfortable; others want to help their friends, still others want to "do many good deeds" with the money which is not theirs. Rent-seeking, abuse of influence, distribution of "favours" and the like are common. They are all the more likely to prevail if the roles vis-à-vis the institution are not well-defined and not clearly separated. A carefully devised "constitution" which also clearly distinguishes roles is crucial in order to limit abuses. It contains checks and balances and assigns powers and responsibilities.

Although there are no universally applicable rules for drafting the constitution of a development institution, the following principles have emerged as quite general and important.

Most important is a clearcut division of functions between the management and a policy-setting and supervising body which will henceforth be called the directorate. The management is solely responsible for running the institution according to the general guidelines laid down and supervised by the directorate and under the supervision of the directorate.

There are several reasons for this separation of roles, which corresponds to the German system of management board and supervisory board and is partially in contrast to the American system based on a board of directors: A well-defined degree of autonomy for management is a form of protection against undue intervention in important decisions in matters such as the recruitment of personnel, granting loans and enforcing repayment. Since they are not involved in day-to-day business, outside directors might have a tendency to intervene in these decisions for largely personal reasons. Management autonomy is an indispensible requirement if the management is held responsible for what it does or fails to do. In addition, the management can only develop a sense of operational efficiency, a long-term perspective and professionalism if its powers and duties are well-defined and if it does not need to worry about being fired because it protects the institution from undue influence by the directors. Since in financial institutions in developing countries, the directors will often be politicians, a largely autonomous management would seem to be necessary for the institution's survival.

The autonomy of management should be limited by the supervision which is exercised by the directorate. This should help to prevent abuses of power on the part of the management for personal goals. In addition, management is appointed by, and accountable to, the directorate.

This system of checks and balances – the directorate is excluded from operating decisions, and management is monitored by the directorate – can help to prevent a great deal of mismanagement, fraud, self-dealing etc. which are frequently encountered in development finance institutions. This is not sufficient, however. Additional, external controls are needed. They might be provided by a competent bank supervisory body and/or an association. This is one of the reasons why we think that it is very important to make any development finance institution subject to bank supervision as soon as possible and why we regard a strong supervisory authority as a core element of a good financial system. Indeed, donor support to the institution responsible for banking regulation and its enforcement (second-tier institution-building) has proved to be an important step towards first-tier institution-building in the financial sector.

A development finance institution should not restrict itself to lending operations. It should also offer deposit facilities, not only because the target groups need such facilities, but also because it strengthens the system of checks and balances: Managers and directors of deposit-taking institutions are subject to a stronger degree of moral and social pressure, and also are often required to assume stricter legal responsibility if depositors' money is at stake. Moreover, bank supervision, based on capital adequacy rules, diversification requirements and other forms of prudential regulation, is normally stricter – or for that matter, only applicable – if an institution accepts deposits. Furthermore, savings mobilization increases the autonomy of a financial institution and reduces its dependance on external functions.

Viewed from the other side, an elaborate system for the prevention of mismanagement, fraud, excessive risk-taking as well as overly lenient conduct vis-à-vis the clientele of the poor, is necessary to ensure that deposit business can be conducted with the general public. It is simply not acceptable, even with the most noble intentions of supporting poor people in mind, to put the savings of these same people at risk.

The interaction between managers, directors and supervisors and, indirectly, depositors will work in favour of institutional sustainability because it helps to ward off many of the common dangers to financial institutions. Sustainability is a necessary condition for assuring a permanent supply of financial services to the target group. In many cases, however, it is not a sufficient condition because a financial institution can be professional, efficient, stable, honest and even an attractive place for poor people's deposits, and still reduce its target group-orientation. This would be the case if the institution stopped lending to the target groups of the poor, for instance, because they are deemed to be too risky as borrowers. Actually, this is a common pattern of institutional development: A financial institution starts with target group-oriented lending; then it "grows up", becomes more professional and learns about the hazards of lending to the poor, accepts deposits, is subject to regulation and, as a result, ends up lending to a less difficult group of borrowers from the upper middle class.

This raises the most difficult question: Which element of the constitution works to ensure that lending activity with the poorer target groups is maintained?

Unfortunately, there is no general answer to this question. In some cases, however, there is a simple answer. If (1) the financial system is very fragmented, (2) normal banks are so conservative that they avoid the poorer people as customers anyway and (3) the competition from the informal and semi-formal financial sector is weak and (4) high interest margins are permitted, then the market segment of the poorer borrowers may simply be rather profitable and it is likely that a financial institution will stick to its market segment despite higher risks.

In other cases the continuity of the orientation to poorer target groups may be the consequence of the composition of the directorate and, to some extent, of the relevant regulation. We shall now discuss this case, which we regard as empirically more relevant.

Who should be on the supervisory board or directorate? The common understanding in business is that the supervisory board represents the owners. But who are the "true" owners of a development finance institution which has typically been initiated by a government agency or an NGO, has received initial funding (including "equity") from foreign donors, and whose good or bad fortunes have the most direct effect on the customers? The organizer/initiator, the provider of the seed capital and the target groups as the actual residual claimant/risk bearer could all claim to be the "owners" and thus the natural holders of board positions. Even if an "owner" were selected from among these three competing constituencies, it would not solve the problem because the supervisory board is more than a representative body for "owners". It also has a monitoring function. The representatives of all three constituencies are normally not qualified at all to perform this function well. At least as far as efficiency and stability aspects are concerned, the monitoring function has to be delegated to some board members who are particularly qualified in this respect.

In view of these problems we recommend that the directorate be con-stituted in such a way that two functions can be performed at the same time. On the supervisory board there should be both, those who are experts in banking and in monitoring the management, and those who represent the long-term interests of the customers. Ideally, one person may fulfil both functions at the same time. For instance, an experienced development banker may be an expert and an advocate for the borrowers. The crucial factor is this: There must not be a clear preponderance for any one of the two functions, so that the directorate always has to find a compromise between efficiency/stability and target-group orientation. It should be added that foreign donors definitely have a role to play in this context: they may act on behalf of the target groups and safeguard the latter's long-term interests.

If the supervisory board is restricted in its operational functions, is

strengthened in its policy–setting and monitoring functions and is com-
posed according to the principle explained above, it will in fact fill the role
of a *board of trustees.* As such it has a responsibility to the target groups,
but should be independent of short–term interests which might be
expressed on the part of the target population.

In this context it is worthwhile to consider the role of politicians as
board members, and the potential of cooperatives.

Politicians who are representatives of state or local governments are
often appointed to the supervisory boards of target–group–oriented
financial institutions. This is especially likely to be the case if the
institution has been initiated by a government office or if it can in some
other form be considered as "belonging" to a public–sector entity. There
can be no doubt that a public sector representation is legitimate as a
matter of principle. However, it is equally clear that the politician must be
subject to the same limitations of powers to interfere in the normal course
of business as apply to other board members. In consideration of the
structural threats which political interference may pose to an institution,
we think that it is essential that a lending institution does not have a
majority of political appointees on the board. However, if they are in a
minority position, they might even play a positive role in terms of
protecting the viability and autonomy of the institution from other political
pressures.

The idea of regarding the supervisory board as the customers' trustee
naturally brings to mind the concept of a cooperative. In a cooperative the
members are beneficiaries and owners. This is why the legal form of a
cooperative seems to be the ideal solution for the incentive problem and
the problem of finding the adequate governance structure. In some cases,
cooperatives may indeed be a good solution, but in many cases they are
not because of the problems of delegation and monitoring: It is extremely
difficult to make sure that the members of the cooperative who sit on a
supervisory board can act, and are motivated to act, in the long–term
interest of the other members. And secondly they are rarely qualified to
monitor the management if, indeed, there should be a separation of
monitoring and management functions.

In conclusion, it should be emphasized that safeguarding the long–
term interests of the target groups and preserving the stability of the
institution can mean different things in different cases, as will become
immediately clear.

3.3.4 Two Examples of Institutional Restructuring

In order to illustrate the important idea of (re)structuring the constitution of a target–group–oriented financial institution, we give a brief

account of two projects in which we have been involved as consultants.

The first example is the Post Office Savings Bank in Tanzania (TPOSB). This institution, which was until very recently an integral part of the postal system, collects savings and lends the funds to the Treasury. Here collecting savings means providing a deposit facility using the country-wide postal network. This is a valuable service from the standpoint of the general population.

In the case of the TPOSB, however, the deposit service was deficient in terms of both the volume of savings mobilised and the quality of the service provided to the public. Thus, there was apparently much scope for improvement. Technical suggestions on what could and should be done had been put on paper by a long line of foreign, donor financed consultants. They did not lead to any change because, so we believe, they did not address the core problem of TPOSB operations.

In fact, the core problem was an inconsistent incentive structure or an inadequate constitution: The Treasury of Tanzania has a strong motive to see improvements made in deposit services because better-quality service will generate a higher volume of cheap funds for the Treasury. Until recently, however, the Treasury had the motive but no opportunity to take action, because the operational aspects of deposit mobilization are strictly an internal matter for the Tanzania Post and Telecommunications Corporation (TPTC). The TPTC, on the other hand, could easily have induced, or simply instructed, its employees to promote the collection of Post Office savings. But it had no incentive to do so, since it would have had to pass the collected savings on to the Treasury. In other words, the Post had a lever, but lacked the motive.

The solution to this problem is straightforward: Put the decision-making power for savings mobilisation efforts in the hands of the institution which benefits from improved savings mobilisation. Incidently, this requires a fundamental transformation of the Post Office Savings Bank Act, which is the legal basis for the dysfunctional "corporate constitution" of the TPOSB. Two different approaches to "constitutional reform" for the TPOSB are conceivable. Both of them would align decision-making power and responsibilty. It does not matter too much whether the Post (TPTC) becomes entitled to keep the savings its clerks collect at the counter and can use them to finance its urgent investment needs, or whether the Treasury takes over the Post Office Savings Bank which would become a legally separate bank, and buy the services of the postal clerks at the counters all over the country from the TPTC. In both variants, there would suddenly be an economic incentive to see to it that the depositor-customers are well-treated. This would represent a great change, and one which would be of benefit to the customers as well as improve the efficiency of the financial system. A far-reaching "constitutional change" is thus the first and decisive step towards rehabilitating the Postal Bank. Obviously, designing the corporate constitution has far reaching implications for both, the organisational structure and the operational procedures of the institution. Their implementation is the second step of a rehabilitation programme. By now (March 1992), the law has been amended accordingly and the technical project of reorganizing the internal structures and procedures of the Bank is scheduled to start soon.

The second example refers to a system of municipal savings banks (MSBs) in Peru, which has been built up with German technical assistance during the last eight years.

Originally, there was a local pawn shop in Piura, a city in the North of Peru. It belonged to the municipality. In 1984, when the project started up, the pawn shop was transformed into a savings bank which accepts savings deposits and grants small loans. The first few years, the MSB only gave loans against gold as collateral. Later on it started to provide lines of credit to local merchants and small producers. Now there is a network of twelve municipal savings banks operating in the rural areas of Peru. In the course of the project a national association and a central training institute have also been established. The former provides technical support to its members and it defines and enforces general controlling standards throughout the network. Amidst the current banking crisis in Peru, the savings banks are stable and, in fact, are growing vigorously – and they have not lost their target–group orientation. They still grant the type of small loans which people had formerly obtained at much higher costs from the local moneylenders. The economic role of the latter has been vastly reduced as a result.

What are the main features of the constitution of the Peruvian municipal savings banks?

First of all, the banks "belong" to the municipalities. It is a privilege for the municipality to have a "caja municipal", which the citizens regard as a political achievement because it protects them from being exploited by usurers. Therefore, the politicians, who come from various parties in the course of time, tend to view the "cajas" favourably. They have even agreed to provide additional equity capital as soon as the annual balance sheet shows a loss in *real* terms despite a high nominal profit. Political interference is difficult by design. There is a five–member board of directors (directorate) with only two representatives of the city. They are mandated by the city council, with one coming from the party in power and one from the opposition. In most cities, one board member is a priest and one is a representative from the local branch of the Central Bank.

On the board there is clearly an interest in having and keeping the "caja" in operation. Even if anyone wanted to use his influence as a board member to impose a decision on the management, it would be rather difficult for them to do so because the bank would insist on being provided sufficient collateral to back the loan. Moreover, anyone who requests a loan and has the required collateral will get the loan anyway. In a system of collateralized loans, non-payment does not "pay off." So, the lending-process is largely "intervention-proof". In addition, the board cannot intervene in the affairs of management, nor has it tried to do so up to now.

By Latin American standards, the directorate's functions are very restricted in scope. The management, by contrast, is powerful. However, this power cannot be employed excessively without control. As the board's capacity to truly supervise the management is clearly limited, a substitute has been found, and to some extent even created, in the framework of the German technical cooperation project: The Peruvian banking supervisory agency, which has for a certain amount of time been the project partner, has established a department which only monitors compliance with the savings bank law. This law, which was enacted in 1986 and was also an outgrowth of the technical cooperation project, contains very specific and rather restrictive provisions on what the savings banks are allowed to do. On the basis of this law, the "superintendencia" has virtual control over every major development in every individual savings bank. If problems arise in an MSB, the "superintendencia" can call in the association to provide assistance on short notice; and if a bank should want to change its target-group orientation or adopt imprudent lending policies it would require, and probably not obtain, authorisation from the bank supervisors.

Thus, it is essentially the basic organisational structure, or the constitution, which makes the Peruvian savings banks adhere to their original target groups and remain economically stable in what may currently be the most unstable economy in Latin America. As in the case of the TPOSB, a fundamental change has been brought about by passing the law.

However, our emphasis on the legal foundations should not create the impression that legal changes are sufficient. Indeed, it was deemed necessary from the beginning to train the personnel in all aspects of banking, including accounting, deposit and credit business, controlling, and to build a "corporate culture" of being professional and successful "bankers for the poor."

3.4 Pragmatic Aspects from a Donor Perspective

The reorganization of an existing (financial) institution in the course of a development project requires a blueprint for reform and a strategy for its implementation. Basic objectives of such a blueprint, notably long–term viability of the institution and its long–term commitment to serving the target groups, have been discussed in the preceeding sections. The following paragraphs briefly discuss three "strategic" aspects of project design: The sequencing of institution building components during the planning phase of the project, the development of a reliable information and controlling system, and the selection of appropriate counterpart institutions. In all instances we present general recommendations from the policy maker's point of view.

3.4.1 Project Planning: Incentives and Enforcement

Institution building is to a large degree an irreversible process which locks both parties – typically a financial institution and a donor agency – into the project. Once the adjustment has begun, it is both difficult and expensive to stop the collaboration, i.e. to terminate the reorganization effort before the project is completed. As always, lock–ins may have detrimental effects for both parties.

First, it is usually very expensive to make fundamental changes in the corporate constitution or the organizational structure of a financial institution during an ongoing reorganization. As an example, consider the case of the banking department of the state–owned post and telecommunications corporation, which is to supposed to become an autonomous institution in the course of a reorganization. Once the relevant law has been amended by parliament, it is difficult or impossible to redirect the reorganizational process to any significant extent, i.e., to change the basic goal of institutional independence.

Second – and this is a similar case – consider a donor agency undertaking an "irreversible" institution–building project. If the counterpart institution demands a significant change in the structure of an entire development project there is little leverage for the donor to resist these attempts at "re–contracting", because it is difficult to enforce any sanctions.

From the point of view of the donor a simple strategy will help to minimize this re–contracting risk. It requires the sequence of project phases to be arranged in such a way that any (one–sided/biased) lock–in effect (working to the disadvantage of the donor) is avoided. For example, if a reorganization project requires legal adjustments, which must be ratified by parliament, as well as a modification of its accounting procedures then the legal adjustment should be completed (and ratified) before the more technical aspects of accounting reform are implemented.

A reasonable and scheduled sequencing of reorganizational activities facilitates the use of "conditionality" in contracts with counterpart institutions. Establishing in advance both qualitative and quantitative criteria for project progress, where a failure to comply with the plan puts the implementation of the next project phase at risk, can be a powerful instrument to align the incentives of a donor and its counterpart institution for the entire duration of the project. In our experience, a number of scheduled progress reviews and possible "early termination points" – possibly per year – should be provided for in the contracts for long-term projects.

3.4.2   Project Control and Budgeting

In the initial phase of most reorganization projects expatriate advisors often play an important role. The question of whether or not their effort will have a lasting effect on the institution's performance has a lot to do with the quality of controlling to which all relevant activities of the institution are subjected. The establishment of an effective controlling system has two dimensions, one internal and one external to the institution. The former is closely related to the management information system. Its distinctive contribution consists in presenting performance targets at the beginning of every period, and in using them to gauge the success, or the failure, of the institution's management.

Monitoring the performance of a financial institution in terms of economic viability and target group orientation on a continuous basis is strenghtened by external supervision, like that provided by the banking supervisory authority. Although supervisory standards in many countries are relatively lax, it appears to be a reasonable strategy for a project to support the reorganizational effort by training the external controllers. Integrating internal and external control into the reorganization project increases the probability of a lasting impact on the institution and its economic performance.

3.4.3   Selecting Counterpart Institutions

Many financial projects have no designated counterpart institution at the outset. Hence there is search for a suitable, or optimal, intermediary in the initial phase of the project. We advocate investing some time (and money) in this identification process. To a large extent, the potential of the partner institution, and any fundamental constraints, it may face determine the scope for reorganization measures and the probability that they will succeed.

In light of the principal findings presented in previous chapters of the study, we propose a simple technique for the analysis and solution of the problem: each precisely specified project, option or alternative is first evaluated according to a list of criteria or objectives. The resulting criteria-related evaluation in each case is then weighted in line with the importance of the criteria involved. The task of indicating the extent to which a specific project meets a given requirement is a "technical" matter which can, in principle, be delegated, e.g., to a consultant. Assigning weights to the individual criteria, on the other hand, is a task for the decision-making unit itself, as it is responsible for policy-related or value judgements.

We suggest employing a list to consist initially of four criteria (points 1 through 4) to assess the desirability of a given project from the standpoint of development policy (see Table 6). To this basic list, which could be employed by all relevant institutions, criteria for which could be

Criteria	Weight 1	Alternatives			
		RoSCA 2	CC 3	RCF 4	CGF 5
#1 Target Group Orientation					
#2 Sustainability					
#3 Marginal Impact					
#4 Replicability (potential total impact)					
#5 Synergy (for donor)					
#6 Tri--partite component (ILO)					
#7 Innovatism (market niche)					
#8 Resource Requirements ("Small is beautifull")					
Evaluation Index (weighted sum)	1,0				

1) Relative Importance of criteria #1 through #8, adding up to 1
2) RoSCA - Rotating Savings and Credit Association
3) CC - Credit Cooperative
4) RCF - Revolving Credit Fund
5) CGF - Credit Guarantee Fund

Table 6:   Decision matrix comprising four general development economic criteria plus four donor-specific (here: ILO) criteria

employed by all relevant institutions, criteria for specific donors or implementing agencies can be added. By means of an example we have completed the matrix with four criteria (5 through 8) which might be specific to ILO as the relevant donor or implementing agency.

1) *Target group orientation* is the indicator of a project's ability to reach the poorer strata of the population. It is closely related to the idea of banking for the poor.

2) *Sustainability* refers to the ability of a financial institution to supply its financial services on a permanent basis. This implies that operations have to be profitable or must at least cover all costs, including capital costs, adjusted for inflation. Over the medium term, a project that is sustainable will not have to rely on subsidies from the national government or on foreign experts and infusions of foreign capital. Sustainability depends critically on the financial institutions' ability to mobilize savings and to allocate them wisely and safely.

3) The *marginal impact* represents an estimate of the welfare contribution at the level of its customers which is made possible by the project itself.

4) *Replicability* is a proxy for the potential impact which the project might have on the economy. It involves the question of whether experience is gained or a new concept is developed in the course of a project that can later be imitated (not necessarily by foreign donors) on a much larger scale.

5) The *synergy* between a finance project under consideration and other donor activities measures the extent to which the know–how and other resources which are already available can be utilized in the sense of producing economies of scope. Obviously, the donors may also profit from "learning curve" effects and other transaction cost economies.

6) The *tri-partite concept*, which is characteristic of ILO and some of its projects, refers to the mutual efforts of employers, employees and the government, and is seen as a desirable project characteristic. It would appear to be desirable for finance projects undertaken by ILO to be designed in such a way that the three parties can pool their efforts for the benefit of the target groups.

7) The idea of project *marketing* is considered to be a serious subject today. We interpret it to mean that a project must have some innovative, non–standard features to offer if it is to be attractive to a potential donor. Ideally, a new project should fill a market niche, from the standpoint of both project design and demand by the target group.

8) The *resource requirement* summarizes the flow of financial and technical resources that are needed to achieve the project

objective. It includes a time dimension, as many projects have a long start–up phase. Other things being equal, a project with a low resource requirement will always be more attractive.

Table 6 lists these eight criteria on the vertical axis (row 2 through 9). The first row is reserved for the project alternatives which are to be compared. Those listed in Table 6 are, of course, only examples. The alternative "RoSCA" could be a project to spread the concept into areas where it has not yet been employed. The alternatives in row 1 may either be specific projects – such as support to a specific CC or cooperative system. But the planning matrix could also be applied for a pre–selection of types of projects which a donor institution may want to start supporting.

An evaluation number or score can be entered in each field of the matrix to indicate the extent to which a certain alternative (= column) meets a specific criterion (= row). The alternatives may be ranked on a scale of 1 (poor) to 5 (very positive). Although filling in the numbers in the cells of the matrix is a "technical" task which can be delegated, as we have already mentioned, neither the selection of criteria to be employed, nor, of course, the compilation of the list of projects or options to be evaluated can easily be delegated. This is particularly true with regard to the most important step, namely that of weighting the criteria. This step cannot be delegated. A suitable value function, to be entered in the second column, assigns (relative) weights to the eight criteria. Individual weights should range between zero (irrelevant) and one (very important), and the sum of all weights must be one. When the list has been completed up to this point, the alternatives can be ranked according to the weighted sum of the respective scores.

F

SUMMARY AND OUTLOOK

This chapter begins with a concise summary – presented in the form of 20 propositions – of what we consider to be the essence of the preceding chapters. In the next and final section we offer some suggestions concerning an agenda for further research, notably for empirical studies about governance structures of development finance institutions including credit cooperatives and non–profit organizations.

1. A Summary in the Form of 20 Propositions

Chapter B on finance and development provides an overview of how the role attributed to finance in the process of economic development has changed over time. Whereas in early thinking finance was perceived as a homogenous input in an aggregate production function, it is seen nowadays as a set of institutions that provide infrastructural support for economic development. From a development finance perspective, the quality of the services or functions performed by the financial infrastructure is more relevant than the sheer quantity of capital accumulated and allocated.

1) Finance contributes to development through intermediation and transformation of capital in terms of lot size, term structure and risk.

2) There is a considerable demand for financial services on the part of the poorer segments of the population in developing countries, particularly as far as permanent access to fairly priced credit and to deposit facilities with low transaction costs is concerned.

3) The provision of financial services to a broad segment of the population is possible on a sustainable, cost–covering basis,

provided that the regulatory environment is not too unfavourable. However, this presupposes that those who design and implement target group oriented finance projects embrace a concept of banking for the poor that is based on serious and strictly enforced banking practices, instead of a "soft" approach which amounts to the provision of social services.

4) Development projects in support of finance should consist primarily of technical assistance in the sense of support for institution building (rather than financial assistance).

Chapter C shows how financial dualism ("coexistence" of formal and informal sector activities) is an outgrowth of the accessibility of a country's legal infrastructure.

5) Financial arrangements in the informal sector are self-enforcing, i.e. they do not have to avail themselves of the services of the legal infrastructure.

6) Having to rely on self-enforcing informal financial arrangements typically gives rise to either a sequence of contracts (reciprocity) or multiple contracts (interlinked transactions).

7) Adopting some of the methods and policies of informal finance can benefit formal financial institutions if they attempt to reach and serve clients in the informal sector (households, small-scale enterprises, informal financial institutions). For that matter, there is something to be learned from informal financial practices in terms of lowering costs and inducing borrowers to repay loans.

8) Informal financial institutions themselves exhibit little potential as beneficiaries of outside assistance, in particular there is not much to be gained from linking them to formal-sector institutions.

Chapter D develops a framework for an economic analysis of financial institutions, concentrating on their governance structure. The emphasis is on the financial and the organizational efficiency of various financial institutions, such as rotating savings and credit associations, rotating credit funds, postal banks, and credit guarantee funds, and on the links between financial and organizational efficiency in these institutions.

9) Any stable financial arrangement, be it formal or informal, can be analyzed in terms of its governance structure, or corporate constitution. The term governance structure refers to the

allocation of decision–making powers among all parties involved (owners, managers, regulators, members/customers) and the limitations to which their powers are subject (legislation, supervision, social norms).

10) Over the long term, the objectives of an organization such as a financial institution are not imposed by fiat, but are the result of its governance structure. Therefore, if a financial institution is to be oriented, and remain oriented, towards serving poor customers, the governance structure has to be designed accordingly.

11) The operational efficiency of a financial institution in the formal, semi–formal and informal financial sectors is also determined by the soundness of its governance structure. Here, soundness means the provision of incentives that will motivate the individual actors to behave in such a way that the institution remains viable over the long term.

12) There is a symbiotic relationship between target–group–oriented credit and deposit business: Providing deposit services meets an essential demand on the part of poor people and helps to stabilize a given financial institution.

13) The economic value of the financial services offered by rotating savings and credit associations (RoSCAs) is quite limited. By comparison, the services which could be offered by a credit cooperative would be more valuable. A credit cooperative is able to fulfill the functions of intermediation and transformation to a much larger extent.

14) On the other hand, the soundness of the RoSCA's governance structure is impressive, whereas credit cooperatives tend to suffer from serious dysfunctional characteristics. Consequently, credit cooperatives do not live up to their founders' expectations and operate well below their economic potential.

15) Group lending, which is not a financial institution in its own right, but rather a financial technique, utilizes the idea of reciprocity in the form of mutual liability to increase the creditworthiness of an informal clientele. However, the quality of its risk–sharing properties is inherently poor and the scope for transaction–cost economies is limited.

Chapter E discusses the methodological aspects of financial institution–building and takes the relevant structural parameters of an economy, especially the progress that has been made in the area of general economic reform, as its starting point. The focus is on ways and means of enhancing target group orientation and increasing stability, both with respect to financial services and to the incentives that are in place for management.

16) A liberalized formal financial market may be a necessary condition for the creation of a spontaneous supply of financial services to the target group, but in itself it is not sufficient to achieve this effect. Consequently, there is a need for intervention and technical assistance, even if "financial repression" has been abolished.

17) Generally speaking, there is some scope for intervention in informal financial arrangements and institutions, but the replicability and impact of such measures will probably be rather limited.

18) Upgrading, downgrading and linking neither represent a complete set of possible innovative project strategies, nor are they mutually exclusive alternatives.

19) For financial institutions in the formal and informal sectors, upgrading in the sense of increasing the degree of formality is in most cases an essential step towards enhancing their stability. The latter itself is a necessary condition for the institution to maintain its target–group orientation over the long term. Hence, upgrading should be a part of most, if not all, programmes and projects geared to improving financial sector performance.

20) Assistance should never be provided to a financial arrangement or an institution which is not expected to become self-sustaining (i.e. viable and durable) after a limited start up-phase. In other words: "Just say NO ... to money–losing credit projects" (J.D. Von Pischke).

2. Outlook

The last decade has experienced a profound change of how finance is considered to be related to, and relevent for, economic development. We have presented our view on the subject in the foregoing chapters. Given the complexities of institutional forms and of regulating constraints, there will be hardly any room for "cookbook"-type of solutions, or standardized optimal forms. Today, there is little factual knowledge about observable institutional conditions that explain financial performance and long–term survival of financial institutions in developing countries.

The next step towards a deeper understandimg of institutional development will, in our opinion, consist in the attempt to gather evidence on how financial institutions, especially intermediaries, do cope with the incentive problems inherent in their respective organizational structure.

By means of selected examples we will point to a couple of possible research areas, all of which require a combined effort of theoretical and empirical work. Our sample of research questions relates to credit cooperatives, rotating credit funds, non-profit institutions, and commercial banks.

(1) Credit cooperatives

(1.1) An economic analysis of selected credit cooperatives

In line with our principal hypothesis with regard to the importance of a financial institution's internal, or organizational, efficiency for its performance as a target group oriented institution, an in-depth study should be undertaken to investigate the governance structure of individual credit cooperatives, including the relationship between this structure and financial performance. In order to ensure the validity of the conclusions to be drawn from this type of investigation, the methodology used to analyze the governance structure and evaluate financial performance has to be standardized for all studies undertaken.

(1.2) Credit cooperatives and the multi-tier system

The organizational and financial performance of a primary credit cooperative may depend on the activities of the regional or national "layers" of the cooperative system. The widespread three-tier system in this sector can be analyzed along much the same lines as in Research Project 1.1 above. This study might also provide an answer to the question of which counterpart "layer" - the primary, secondary or tertiary cooperatives - would be most appropriate for institution-building support in the future.

(1.3) Identifying synergies in multi-purpose cooperatives

This study, which could also build on the findings of Research Project 1.1, should examine the tenability of a widespread belief concerning MPCs, namely, that the combination of different sectoral activities under the roof of a single cooperative (e.g., input delivery, output marketing, and credit granting) improves the institution's efficiency and helps to overcome the incentive problems between the cooperative as a lending institution and its borrowers.

(2) Economic analysis of selected non-profit organizations (NPOs)

It is a widely held belief that non–profit organizations (sometimes also called non–governmental organizations, NGOs) have less incentive problems than for–profits, because their members and management are intrinsically motivated and therefore better suited to maintain a desired target group orientation. Empirical evidence will probably challenge this optimistic view. Again, the strengths and weaknesses of specific NPO constitutions have to be investigated using a methodology similar to that employed in Research Project 1.1. The underlying objective is to draw conclusions concerning the quality of NPO governance structures, to learn methods of improving their (economic) stability, and to test the hypothesis that a NPO is an efficient organizational form, provided its production process displays a high degree of quality uncertainity (Weisbrod, 1988). It deserves mention that NPOs are of special interest to the development economist, both from a theoretical and a pragmatic perspective. Although NPOs play a significant role in development finance, there are few detailed studies on the incentive and control issue of these institutions.

(3) Revolving credit funds (RCFs)

RCFs are usually set up to support the clientele of other development projects (often agricultural or infrastructural) by means of credit. Available evidence suggests that RCFs have missed their objectives by a very wide margin (ILO, 1991). An inconsistent governance structure diluting the economic differences between loans and grants explains probably most of the observable inefficiency.

(3.1) Upgrading or formalizing RCFs

How is it possible to transform an existing RCF into an institution with survival value, i.e. an institution with a well–conceived corporate constitution?

(3.2) Linking RCFs

If an RCF is too small to become an independent financial institution, how can it be attached to an institution that already exists, e.g. a commercial bank? If such a project is to be implemented, advisory assistance must include the creation of an information system through which it is possible to monitor effectively the fund's performance in terms of both financial viability and target group orientation.

(4) Commercial banks

In liberalized financial markets, i.e. ones in which financial repression has been eliminated, one should take a fresh look at commmercial banks, private and public, and their potential as managers of *dedicated* revolving funds. Relevant experiences should be collected and surveyed to determine the kind of regulatory regime and the kind of contractual conditions that are required to induce a commercial bank to increase not only lending to microenterprises "at the margin" but also savings mobilization.

(5) Formalization of semi-formals

Evidence should be collected and evaluated which would demonstrate the success or failure of attempts to stabilize semi-formal financial institutions by formalizing them, i.e. by making them subject to supervision by the national banking authorities. Furthermore, the formalization process should be analyzed and appropriate policy conclusions presented.

These five groups of proposals are extremely tentative in nature. We have presented them because, as we have sought to demonstrate in this study, we believe that it is very important to learn much more about these questions than development experts/consultants and the academic communities seem to know at the present time. This kind of research would immediately help to improve project design. However, we do not suggest a sequence of steps which begins with research, generates results, and then leads to project design. Rather, we suggest setting up "joint projects", i.e. assistance projects which contain the type of research we advocate as an important element. Indeed, other than in the context of an ongoing project, the type of research we deem necessary – namely, "action research" – is almost impossible.

BIBLIOGRAPHY

ADAMS, Dale W. (1978): Mobilizing Household Savings through Rural Financial Markets, *Economic Development and Cultural Change*, Vol. 26, pp. 547-560

ADAMS, Dale W. (1992): Taking a Fresh Look at Informal Finance, in: Adams, D. W.; Fitchett D.A. (eds.): *Informal Finance in Low-Income Countries*, Boulder: Westview Press, pp. 5-23

ADAMS, Dale W.; ANTONIO, Alfredo; ROMERO, Pablo (1981): Group Lending to the Rural Poor in the Dominican Republic: A Stunted Innovation, *Canadian Journal on Agricultural Economics*, Vol. 29, pp. 216-224

ADAMS, Dale W; FITCHETT, Delbert A. (eds.) (1992): *Informal Finance in Low-Income Countries*, Boulder: Westview Press, pp. 195-208,

ADAMS, Dale W.; GRAHAM, Douglas H. (1981): A Critique of Traditional Agricultural Credit Projects and Policies, *Journal of Development Economics*, Vol. 8, pp. 347-366

ADAMS, Dale W.; GRAHAM, Douglas H.; VON PISCHKE, J.D. (eds.) (1984): *Undermining Rural Development with Cheap Credit*, Boulder: Westview Press

ADAMS, Dale W.; VOGEL, Robert C. (1986): Rural Financial Markets in Low-Income Countries: Recent Controversies and Lessons, *World Development*, Vol.14, pp. 447-487

ADAMS, Dale W.; VON PISCHKE, J. D. (1990): Microenterprise Credit Programs: Déjà Vu, mimeo, Washington, D.C.

ADELMAN, Irma; MORRIS, Cynthia (1968): Performance Criteria for Evaluating Economic Development Potential: An Operational Approach, *Quarterly Journal of Economics*, Vol. 92, pp. 260-280

AKERLOF, George (1976): The Economics of Caste and of the Rat Race and Other Woeful Tales, *Quarterly Journal of Economics*, Vol. 90, pp. 599-617

ARMBRUSTER, Paul G. (1990): *Finanzielle Infrastruktur und organische Entwicklung durch Genossenschaften in ländlichen Räumen der Dritten Welt*, Göttingen: Vandenhoeck & Ruprecht

ARNDT, Heinz W. (1988): "Market Failure" and Underdevelopment, *World Development*, Vol. 16, pp. 219-229

ASHE, Jeffrey (1985): *The PISCES II Experience: Local Efforts in Micro-Enterprise Development*, Vol. 1, Washington, D.C.: US-Agency for International Development

BALASSA, Bela (1989): Financial Liberalization in Developing Countries, Working Paper, Washington, D.C.: World Bank

BALDUS, Rolf D.; RÖPKE, Jochen; SEMMELROTH, Dieter (1981): *Einkommens-, Verteilungs- und Beschäftigungswirkungen von Selbsthilfeorganisationen in Entwicklungsländern*, Köln: Weltforum-Verlag

BALKENHOL, Bernd (1990): Guaranteeing Bank Loans to Smaller Entrepreneurs in Africa, *International Labour Review*, Vol. 129, pp. 245-253

BALTENSPERGER, Ernst; DEVINNEY, Timothy M. (1985): Credit Rationing Theory: A Survey and Synthesis, *Journal of Institutional and Theoretical Economics*, Vol 141, pp. 475-502

BARDHAN, Pranab (ed.) (1989): *The Economic Theory of Agrarian Institutions*, Oxford: Clarendon Press

BEDARD, Guy (1991): *Development Banking with the Poor, for the Poor and by the Poor: New Models for Banking*, Eschborn: GTZ

BENCIVENGA, Valerie R.; SMITH, Bruce D. (1991): Financial Intermediation and Endogenous Growth, *Review of Economic Studies*, Vol. 58, pp. 195-209

BENTIL, Bernard, et al. (1988): *Rural Finance in Ghana*, Accra/Frankfurt: Interdisziplinäre Projekt Consult

BERNANKE, Ben (1983): Non-Monetary Effects of the Financial Crisis in the Propagation of the Great Depression, *American Economic Review*, Vol 73, pp. 257-276

BERRY, Albert; GOLDMARK, Susan (1988): The Impact of Financial Market Policies: A Review of the Literature and the Empirical Evidence, Bethesda: Development Alternatives, Inc.

BLEJER, Mario; SAGARI, Silvia (1987): The Structure of the Banking Sector and the Sequence of Financial Liberalization, in: Connolly, M.; Gonzalez-Vega, C. (eds.): *Economic Reform and Stabilization in Latin America*, New York: Praeger, pp. 93-110

BMZ-Bundesministerium für wirtschaftliche Zusammenarbeit (1986): Armutsbekämpfung durch Selbsthilfe, Bonn: BMZ

BMZ-Bundesministerium für wirtschaftliche Zusammenarbeit (1989): Ergebnisbericht aus dem Arbeitsschwerpunkt "Sparen und Kredit", Bonn: BMZ/DEG/GTZ/KfW

BONUS, Holger (1986): The Cooperative Association as a Business Enterprise: A Study in the Economics of Transactions, *Journal of Institutional and Theoretical Economics*, Vol. 142, pp. 310-339

BONUS, Holger (1987): Die Genossenschaft als modernes Unternehmenskonzept, Münster: Institut für Genossenschaftswesen

BONUS, Holger; SCHMIDT, Georg (1990): The Cooperative Banking Group in The Federal Republic of Germany: Aspects of Institutional Change, *Journal of Institutional and Theoretical Economics*, Vol. 146, pp. 180-207

BOOMGARD, James (1989): Microenterprise Stock-Taking: Synthesis Report. *AID-Evaluation Special Studies* 65, Washington, D.C.: US-Agency for International Development

BOOMGARD, James J.; ANGELL, Kenneth J. (1990): Developing Financial Services for Microenterprises: An Evaluation of USAID Assistance to the BRI Unit Desa System in Indonesia, *GEMINI Technical Report* No. 6, Bethesda: Development Alternatives, Inc.

BOUMAN, F. J. A. (1977): Indigenous Savings and Credit Societies in the Third World: A Message, *Savings and Development*, Vol. 1, pp. 181-214

BOUMAN, F. J. A. (1989): *Small, Short and Unsecured*, Delhi: Oxford University Press

BRATTON, Michael (1986): Financing Smallholder Production: A Comparison of Individual and Group Credit Schemes in Zimbabwe, *Public Adminstration and Development,* Vol. 6, pp. 115-132

BRAVERMAN, Avishay; GUASCH, Luis (1986): Rural Credit Markets and Institutions in Developing Countries: Lessons for Policy Analysis from Practice and Modern Theory, *World Development,* Vol. 14, pp. 1253-1267

BRAVERMAN, Avishay; GUASCH, Luis (1989): Rural Credit Reforms in LDCs: Issues and Evidence, *Journal of Economic Development,* Vol. 14, pp. 7-33

BRAVERMAN, Avishay; GUASCH, Luis (1989a): Institutional Analysis of Credit Co-operatives, in: Bardhan, P. (ed.): *The Economic Theory of Agrarian Institutions,* Oxford: Clarendon Press, pp. 340-355

BRAVERMAN, Avishay; STIGLITZ, Joseph E. (1982): Sharecropping and the Interlinking of Agrarian Markets, *American Economic Review,* Vol. 72, pp. 695-715

BRAVERMAN, Avishay; STIGLITZ, Joseph E. (1986): Landlords, Tenants, and Technological Innovations, *Journal of Development Economics,* Vol 23, pp. 313-332

BROWN, David, L.; KORTEN, David L. (1989): Understanding Voluntary Organizations: Guidelines for Donors, Working Paper, Washington, D.C.: World Bank

BRUNO, Michael (1988): Opening up: Liberalization with Stabilization, in: Dornbusch, R.; Leslie, F.; Helmers C.H. (eds.): *The Open Economy: Tools for Policymakers in Developing Countries,* New York: Oxford University Press, pp. 223-247

CAMERON, Rondo (1967): *Banking in the Early Stages of Industrialization: A Study in Comparative Economic History,* New York: Oxford University Press

CHANDAVARKAR, Anand G. (1985): The Non-Institutional Financial Sector in Developing Countries: Macroeconomic Implications for Savings Policies, *Savings and Development,* Vol. 8, pp. 129-141

CHANDAVARKAR, Anand G. (1989): Informal Credit Markets in Support of Microbusiness, in: Levitsky, J. (ed.), *Microenterprises in Developing Countries*, London: Intermediate Technology Publications, pp. 79-96

CHENERY, Hollis; STROUT, Alan M. (1966): Foreign Assistance and Economic Development, American Economic Review, Vol. 56, pp. 679-733

CHO, Yoon Je (1986): Inefficiencies from Financial Liberalization in the Absence of Well-Functioning Equity Markets, *Journal of Money, Credit and Banking*, Vol. 18, pp. 191-199

COOPER, R. (1984): On Allocative Distortions in Problems of Self-Section, *Rand Journal of Economics*, Vol. 15, pp. 568-577

CORSEPIUS, Uwe (1988): Interest Rate Reform and Private Investment Behaviour in Developing Countries. Evidence from Peru, Kiel: Institut für Weltwirtschaft

CUEVAS, Carlos E. (1988): Transaction Costs of Financial Intermediation in Developing Countries, Columbus: Ohio State University

DATTA-CHAUDHURI, Mrinal (1990): Market Failure and Government Failure, *Journal of Economic Perspectives*, Vol. 4, Summer, pp. 25-39

DESAI, B.M. (1983b): Group Lending in Rural Areas, in: Von Pischke, J.D.; Adams, D. W.; Donald, G. (eds.): *Rural Financial Markets in Developing Countries;* Baltimore/London: Johns Hopkins University Press, pp. 284-288

DESCHAMPS, Jean-Jaques (1989): Credit for the Rural Poor. The Experience in Six African Countries: Synthesis Report, Bethesta: Development Alternatives, Inc.

DESCHAMPS, Jean-Jaques; GRANT, William (1988): The Impact of Financial Market Policies: A Review of the Literature and the Empirical Evidence, Bethesda: Development Alternatives, Inc.

DIAMOND, Douglas W. (1984): Financial Intermediation and Delegated Monitoring, *Review of Economic Studies*, Vol. 51, pp. 393-414

DIAZ-ALEJANDRO, Carlos (1985): Good-Bye Financial Repression, Hello Financial Crash, *Journal of Development Economics*, Vol. 19, pp. 1-24

DORNBUSCH, Rüdiger (1990): From Stabilization to Growth, *NBER Working Paper*, Cambridge, Mass.: NBER

DORNBUSCH, Rüdiger; REYNOSO, Alejandro (1989): Financial Factors in Economic Development, *American Economic Review, Papers and Proceedings*, Vol. 79, pp. 204-209

DÜLFER, Eberhard (1984): *Betriebwirtschaftslehre der Kooperative*, Göttingen: Vandenhoeck & Ruprecht

EASLEY, David; O'HARA, Maureen (1983): The Economic Role of the Nonprofit Firm, *Bell Journal of Economics*, Vol. 14, pp. 531-538

EGGER, Philippe (1986): Banking for the Rural Poor: Lessons from some Innovative Savings and Credit Schemes, *International Labour Review*, Vol. 125, pp. 447-462

ELKJAER, Joergen (1990): The Cooperative Banking Group in the Federal Republic of Germany: Aspects of Institution Change - Comment, *Journal of Institutional and Theoretical Economics*, Vol. 146, pp. 208-210

ELWERT, Georg; EVERS, Hans-Dieter; WILKENS, Werner (1983): Die Suche nach Sicherheit: Kombinierte Produktionsformen im sogenannten Informellen Sektor, *Zeitschrift für Soziologie*, Vol. 12, pp. 281-296

FAMA, Eugene; JENSEN, Michael (1983): Separation of Ownership and Control, *Journal of Law and Economics*, Vol. 26, pp. 301-326

FAMA, Eugene (1985): What's Different about Banks?, *Journal of Monetary Economics*, Vol. 15, pp. 29-39

FARBMAN, Michael (ed.) (1981): *The PISCES Studies: Assisting the Smallest Economic Activities of the Urban Poor*, Washington, D.C.: US-Agency for International Development

FISCHER, Bernhard (1982): *Liberalisierung der Finanzmärkte und wirtschaftliches Wachstum in Entwicklungsländern*, Tübingen: J.C.B. Mohr

FRY, Maxwell (1988): *Money, Interest and Banking in Economic Development*, Baltimore/London: Johns Hopkins University Press

GALBIS, Vincente (1986): Financial Sector Liberalization under Oligopolistic Conditions and a Bank Holding Company Structure, *Savings and Development*, Vol. 10, pp. 117-140

GEIS, Heinz-Günter (1975): Die Rolle der finanziellen Infrastruktur bei der Kapitalbildung, in: Priebe, H. (ed), *Eigenfinanzierung der Entwicklung*, Berlin: Duncker & Humblot, pp. 69-78

GERMIDIS, Dimitri; KESSLER, Denis; MEGHIR, Rachel (1991): *Financial Systems and Development: What Role for the Formal and Informal Financial Sectors?* Paris: OECD

GERTLER, Mark (1988): Financial Structure and Aggregate Economic Activity: An Overview, *Journal of Money, Credit and Banking*, Vol.20, pp. 559-588

GOLDSMITH, Raymond W. (1969): *Financial Structure and Economic Development*, New Haven: Yale University Press

GOLDMAN, Morrris B. (1984): The United States Treasury Review of the Multilateral Development Banks, *Journal of Monetary Economics 13*, Vol. 13, pp. 275-293

GONZALEZ-VEGA, Claudio (1984), "Credit-Rationing Behavior of Agricultural Lenders: The Iron Law of Interest-Rate Restrictions", in: Adams D.W.; Graham, D.H.; Von Pischke, J.D. (eds.): *Undermining Rural Development with Cheap Credit*, Boulder: Westview Press, pp. 78-95

GONZALEZ-VEGA, Claudio (1986): The Ohio State University's Approach to Rural Financial Markets, Columbus: Ohio State University

GONZALEZ-VEGA, Claudio (1988): Rural Deposit Mobilization in the Dominican Republic, Washington, D.C.: World Bank

134

GREENWALD, Bruce; **STIGLITZ**, Joseph. E. (1989): Information, Finance and Markets: The Architecture of Allocative Mechanisms, Working Paper, Stanford University, forthcoming in *Journal of Industrial and Corporate Change*

GURLEY, John. G.; **SHAW**, Edward. S. (1955): Financial Aspects of Economic Development, *American Economic Review*, Vol. 45, pp. 515-538

GURLEY, John. G.; **SHAW**, Edward. S. (1960): *Money in the Theory of Finance*, Washington, D.C.: Brookings Institution

GURLEY, John. G.; **SHAW**, Edward. S. (1967): Financial Structure and Economic Development, in: *Economic Development and Cultural Change*, Vol. 15, pp. 257-268

HANKEL, Wilhelm (1990): Kapitalmärkte und Finanzinstitutionen im Entwick-lungsprozeß, in: Körner, H. (ed.): *Zur Analyse von Institutionen im Entwicklungsprozeß und in der internationalen Zusammenarbeit*, Berlin: Duncker & Humblot, pp. 169-202

HART, Keith (1973): Informal Income Opportunities and Urban Employment in Ghana, *The Journal of Modern African Studies*, Vol. 11, pp. 61-89

HARTIG, Peter (1989): *Kleinbäuerliche Kreditprogramme und Institution-Building auf ländlichen Finanzmärkten in Entwicklungsländern*, Offenbach: Falk

HIRSCHMAN, Albert O. (1984): *Getting Ahead Collectively: Grassroots Experiences in Latin America*, Elmsford, N.Y.: Pergamon Press

HOFF, Karla; **STIGLITZ**, Joseph E. (1990): Introduction: Imperfect Information and Rural Credit Markets - Puzzles and Policy Perspectives, *World Bank Research Observer*, Vol. 4, pp. 235-269

HOLMSTRÖM, Bengt R.; **TIROLE**, Jean (1989): The Theory of the Firm, in: Schmalensee, R.; Willig, R. D. (eds.), *Handbook of Industrial Organization*, Vol. 1, Amsterdam: North Holland, pp. 61-134

HOLT, Sharon (1991): The Role of Institutions in Poverty Reduction, Washington, D.C.: World Bank

HOLT, Sharon (1991a): Village Banking: A Cross-Country Study of a Community-Based Lending Methodology, Washington, D.C.: World Bank

HOLT, Sharon; RIBE, Helena (1991): Developing Financial Institutions for the Poor and Reducing Barriers to Access for Women, Washington, D.C.: World Bank

HOSSAIN, Mahabub (1988): Credit for Allevation of Rural Poverty: The Grameen Bank in Bangladesh, Washington, D.C.: International Food Policy Research Institute

HUPPI, Monika; FEDER, Gershon (1989): The Role of Groups and Credit Cooperatives in Rural Lending, Washington, D.C.: World Bank

HUPPI, Monika; FEDER, Gershon (1990): Cooperatives in Rural Lending, *World Bank Research Oberserver*, Vol. 5, pp. 187-204

INTERNATIONAL LABOUR OFFICE (1972): *Employment, Income and Equality: A Strategy for Increasing Productive Employment in Kenya*, Geneva: ILO

INTERNATIONAL LABOUR OFFICE (1991): Review of ILO Projects with Financial Components (Draft), Geneva: ILO

ISRAELSEN, L. Dwight (1980): Collectives, Communes, and Incentives, *Journal of Comparative Economics*, Vol. 4, pp. 99-124

JACKELEN, Henry R. (1989): Banking on the Informal Sector, in: Levitsky, J. (ed.): *Microenterprises in Developing Countries*, London: Intermediate Technology Publications, pp. 131-143

JACKELEN, Henry R.; RHYNE, Elisabeth (1991): Toward a more Market-oriented Approach to Credit and Savings for the Poor, mimeo, Washington, D.C.

JENSEN, Michael C.; MECKLING, William H. (1976): Theory of the Firm: Managerial Behavior, Agency Costs, and Ownership Stucture, *Journal of Financial Economics*, Vol. 3, pp. 305-360

KHATKHATE, Deena R. (1988): Assessing the Impact of Interest Rates in Less Developed Countries, *World Development*, Vol. 16, pp. 577-588

KHATKHATE, Deena R.; RIECHEL, Klaus-Walther (1980): Multipurpose Banking: Its Nature, Scope, and Relevance for Less Developed Countries, *International Monetary Fund Staff Papers*, Vol. 27, pp. 478-516

KIRCHNER, Christian (1990): The Cooperative Banking Group in the Federal Republic of Germany: Aspects of Institutional Change - Comment, *Journal of Institutional and Theoretical Economics*, Vol 146, pp. 211-215

KOTLER, Philip; ROBERTO, Eduardo (1989): *Social Marketing*, New York: Free Press

KRAHNEN, Jan Pieter; MERAN, Georg (1987): Why Leasing?, An Introduction to Comperative Contractual Analysis, in: Bamberg, G.; Spremann, K. (eds).: *Agency Theory, Information and Incentives*, Berlin *et al.*: Springer, pp. 255-280

KRAHNEN, Jan Pieter; NITSCH, Manfred (1987): *Kredit und informeller Sektor: Theoretische und empirische Überlegungen zur Konstruktion eines angepaßten Kreditprogramms*, Frankfurt: Interdisziplinäre Projekt Consult

KROPP, Erhard, *et al.* (1989): *Linking Self-help Groups and Banks in Developing Countries*, Eschborn: GTZ

KÜCK, Marlene (1989): *Betriebswirtschaft der Kooperative - Eine einzelwirtschaftliche Analyse kooperativer und selbstverwalteter Betriebe*, Stuttgart: Poeschel

LELE, Uma (1981): Co-operatives and The Poor: A Comparative Perspective, *World Development*, Vol. 9, pp. 55-72

LEVITSKY, Jacob (1986): World Bank Lending to Small Enterprises: A Review, Washington, D.C.: World Bank

LEVITSKY, Jacob (ed.) (1989): *Microenterprises in Developing Countries*, London: Intermediate Technology Publications

LEVITSKY, Jacob; PRASAD, Ranga (1986): Credit Guarantee Schemes for Small and Medium Enterprises, Washington, D.C./ London: World Bank / ODA

LONG, Millard (1983): Review of Financial Sector Work, Washington, D.C.: World Bank

MAGILL, John H. (1984): Cooperatives in Development: A Review Based on the Experiences of U.S. Cooperative Development Organizations, Vol. 1, Bethesda: Development Alternatives, Inc.

MAGILL, John H. (1991): Credit Unions: A Formal Sector Alternative for Financing Microenterprise Development, Bethesda: Development Alternatives, Inc.

MANN, Charles K.; GRINDLE, Merilee S.; SHIPTON, Parker (eds.) (1989): *Seeking Solutions: Framework and Cases for Small Enterprise Development Programs*, West Hartford: Kumarian Press

MARION, Peter J. (1987): Building Successful Financial Systems: The Role of Credit Unions in Financial Sector Development, Washington, D.C.: World Council of Credit Unions

MARION, Peter J. (1990): Credit Union Achievements in Developing Countries, in: *Yearbook of Co-operative Enterprise 1990*, Madison: World Council of Credit Unions, pp. 35-52

MASULIS, Ronald W. (1987): Changes in Ownership Structure: Conversions of Mutual Savings and Loans to Stock Charter, *Journal of Financial Economics*, Vol. 18, pp. 29-59

MAYER, Colin (1987): The Assessment: Financial Systems and Corporate Investments, *Oxford Review of Economic Policy*, Vol. 3, pp. 1-16

MAYERS, David; SMITH, Clifford W. (1988): Ownership Structure across Lines of Property-Casualty Insurance, *Journal of Law and Economics*, Vol. 31, pp. 351-378

McKINNON, Ronald I. (1973): *Money and Capital in Economic Development*, Washington, D.C.: Brookings Institution

McKINNON, Ronald I. (ed.) (1976): *Money and Finance in Economic Growth and Development*, New York: Marcel Dekker

McKINNON, Ronald I. (1986): Financial Liberalization in Retrospect: Interest Rate Policies in LDCs, in: Ranis, G.; Schultz, P. (eds.): *The*

State of Development Economics, New York: Basil Blackwell, pp. 386-410

McKINNON, Ronald I. (1989): Macroeconomic Instability and Moral Hazard in Banking in a Liberalizing Economy, in: Brock, P. L.; Connolly, M. B.; Gonzalez-Vega, C. (eds.): *Latin American Debt and Adjustment*, New York: Praeger, pp. 99-111

McKINNON, Ronald I. (1991): *The Order of Economic Liberalization: Financial Control in the Transition to Market Economy*, Baltimore/London: Johns Hopkins University Press

MERAN, Georg; WOLFSTETTER, Elmar (1987): Optimal Risk Shifting vs. Efficient Employment in Illyria: The Labour Managed Firm under Asymmetric Information, in: *Journal of Comparative Economics*, Vol. 11, pp. 163-179

MEYER, Richard L. (1988): The Viability of Rural Financial Institutions and the System as a Whole, in: *Fourth Technical Consultation on the Scheme for Agricultural Credit Development*, Rome: FAO, pp. 41-44

MEYER, Richard L. (1989): Financial Services for Microenterprises: Programmes or Markets? in: Levitsky, J. (ed.): *Microenterprises in Developing Countries*, London: Intermediate Technology Publications, pp. 121-130

MODIGLIANI, Franco; MILLER, M.H. (1958): The Cost of Capital, Corporation Finance, and the Theory of Investment, *American Economic Review*, Vol. 48, pp. 261-297

NAYAR, C. P. S. (1992): Strengths of Informal Financial Institutions: Examples from India, in : Adams, W.D.; Fitchett, D. A. (eds.): Informal Finance in Low-Income Countries, Boulder: Westview Press

NITSCH, Manfred (1986): "Tödliche Hilfe"? Zur Modifikation der Außenwirtschafts- und Entwicklungstheorie durch die Einbeziehung des Verhaltens von Entwicklungsbürokratien, in: Schmid-Schönbein, T., *et al.* (eds.): *Entwicklungsländer und Weltmarkt. Ökonomie und Gesellschaft, Yearbook 4*, Frankfurt (Main)/New York: Campus, pp. 69-111

139

NITSCH, Manfred (1987): Glaspaläste und Unterentwicklung: Entwicklungsbanken in der Diskussion, Schwefel, D. (ed.): *Soziale Wirkungen von Projekten in der Dritten Welt*, Baden Baden: Nomos, pp. 169-189

NITSCH, Manfred (1990): Vom Nutzen des institutionalistischen Ansatzes für die Entwicklungsökonomie, in: Körner, H. (ed.): *Zur Analyse von Institutionen im Entwicklungsprozeß und in der internationalen Zusammenarbeit*, Berlin: Duncker & Humblot, pp. 37-50; English translation: Reflections on the Usefulness of the Institutionalist Approach to Development Economics, in: *Economics*, Tübingen, Vol. 42, pp. 106-118

NITSCH, Manfred (1991): Sinn und Unsinn von Rotationsfonds in der Kleingewerbe- und Kleinbauernförderung - Ein Beispiel für Angewandte Institutionen-Ökonomik, *Journal für Entwicklungspolitik*, Vol. 1, pp. 41-62

NORTH, Douglas C. (1984): Transaction Costs, Institutions, and Economic History, *Journal of Institutional and Theoretical Economics*, Vol. 140, pp. 7-17

NORTH, Douglas C. (1987): Institutions, Transaction Costs, and Economic Growth, *Economic Inquiry*, Vol. 25, pp. 419-428

O'HARA, Maureen (1981): Property Rights and the Financial Firm, *Journal of Law and Economics*, Vol. 24, pp. 317-332

OTERO, Maria (1986): *El Concepto del Grupo Solidario*, Boston: Acción-AITEC

OTERO, Maria (1988): *Una cuestion de impacto: Los Programas de Grupos Solidarios y su Enfoque hacia la Evaluación*, Tegucigalpa, Honduras: ASEPADE/PACT

PATRICK, Hugh T. (1966): Financial Development and Economic Growth in Developing Countries, *Economic Development and Cultural Change*, Vol. 14, pp. 174-189

PLATTEAU, Jean-Philippe; ABRAHAM, Anita (1986/87): An Inquiry into Quasi-Credit Contracts: The Role of Reciprocal Credit and Interlinked Deals in Small-scale Fishing Communities, *Journal of Development Studies*, Vol. 23, pp. 461-490

PRIEBE, Hermann (ed.) (1975): *Eigenfinanzierung der Entwicklung,* Berlin: Duncker & Humblot

RASMUSEN, Eric (1988): Mutual Banks and Stock Banks, *Journal of Law and Economics,* Vol. 31, pp. 395-421

RHYNE, Elisabeth (1988): The Small Enterprise Approaches to Employment Project: How a Decade of A.I.D. Effort Contributed to the State of Knowledge on Small Enterprise Assistance, Washington, D.C.: US-Agency for International Development

RHYNE, Elisabeth (1991): The Microenterprise Finance Institutions of Indonesia and Their Implications for Donors, Washington, D.C.: Gemini/Development Alternatives , Inc.

RHYNE, Elisabeth; OTERO, Maria (1991): A Financial Systems Approach to Microenterprises, Bethesda: Development Alternatives, Inc.

RIBHEGGE, Hermann (1987): Contestable Markets, Genossenschaften und Transaktionskosten, Münster: Institut für Genossenschaftswesen

ROSE-ACKERMAN, Susan (ed.) (1986): *The Economics of Nonprofit Institutions,* New York: Oxford University Press

SCHMIDT, Reinhard H. (1985): *Small Scale Financing and Credit Intermediaries,* Eschborn: GTZ

SCHMIDT, Reinhard H. (1986): Credit Supply, Self-help, and the Survival of Financial Institutions in Developing Countries, *Jahrbuch für Neue Politische Ökonomie,* Vol. 5, Tübingen: J. C. B. Mohr, pp. 262-279

SCHMIDT, Reinhard H. (1988): Target Group-Oriented Promotion of Rural Finance: The GTZ Approach, in: *Fourth Technical Consultation on the Scheme for Agricultural Credit Development,* Rome: FAO, pp. 30-33

SCHMIDT, Reinhard H.; KROPP, Erhard (1987): *Rural Finance - Guiding Principles,* Eschborn: GTZ

SCHRADER, Heiko (1991): Rotating Savings and Credit Associations - Institutions in the "Middle Rung" of Development? Bielefeld: Universität Bielefeld

SEIBEL, Hans Dieter (1985): Saving for Development. A Linkage Model for Informal and Formal Financial Markets, *Quarterly Journal of International Agriculture*, Vol. 6, pp. 390-398

SEIBEL, Hans Dieter (1989): Linking Informal and Formal Financial Institutions in Africa and Asia, in: Levitsky, J. (ed).): *Microenterprises in Developing Countries*, London: Intermediate Technology Publications, pp. 97-120

SEIBEL, Hans Dieter; KOLL, Michael (1968): *Einheimische Genossenschaften in Afrika*, Düsseldorf: Bertelsmann Universitätsverlag

SEIBEL, Hans Dieter; MARX, Michael T. (1987): *Dual Financial Markets in Africa*, Saarbrücken/Fort Lauderdale: Breitenbach

SHAW, Edward S. (1973): *Financial Deepening in Economic Development*, New York: Oxford University Press

SIDMANN-STEINER, Claudia (1983): Les Associations de Crédit Rotatif: La Banque du Peuple, Diss. Zürich

SIEGERT, Helmut (1987): *Ländliche Entwicklung und Bankpolitik in Entwicklungsländern*, Frankfurt(Main): Peter Lang

SMITH, Bruce D.; STUTZER, Michael J. (1990): Adverse Selection and Mutuality: The Case of the Farm Credit System, *Journal of Financial Intermediation*, Vol. 1, pp. 125-149

SMITH; Bruce D.; STUTZER, Michael J. (1990): Adverse Selection, Aggregate Uncertainty, and the Role for Mutal Insurance Contracts, *Journal of Business*, Vol. 63, pp. 493-510

de SOTO, Hernando (1987): *El Otro Sendero*, Mexico: Editorial Diana, (English version: *The Other Path*, New York: Harper & Row 1989)

de SOTO, Hernando (1989): Structural Adjustment and the Informal Sector, in: Levitsky, J. (ed.), *Microenterprises in Developing Countries*, London: Intermediate Technology Publications, pp. 3-12

STEARNS, Katherine E.: OTERO, Maria (eds.) (1990): *The Critical Connection: Governments, Private Institutions, and the Informal Sector in Latin America*, Washington, D.C.: Acción International

STEARNS, Katherine E. (1991): The Hidden Beast: Delinquency in Microenterprise Credit Programs, *Discussion Paper Series*, Boston: Acción-AITEC

STERN, Nicholas (1989): The Economics of Development: A Survey, *Economic Journal*, Vol. 99, pp. 597-685

STIGLITZ, Joseph E. (1974): Incentives and Risk Sharing in Sharecropping, *Review of Economic Studies*, Vol. 41, pp. 219-255

STIGLITZ, Joseph E. (1985): Credit Markets and the Control of Capital, *Journal of Money, Credit and Banking*, Vol. 17, pp. 133-152

STIGLITZ, Joseph E. (1986): The New Development Economics, *World Development*, Vol. 14, pp. 257-265

STIGLITZ, Joseph E. (1989): Incentives, Information, and Organizational Design, *Empirica*, Vol. 16, pp. 3-29

STIGLITZ, Joseph E. (1989a): Banks versus Markets as Mechanisms for Allocating and Coordinating Investment, mimeo, Stanford

STIGLITZ, Joseph E. (1989b): Markets, Market Failures, and Development, *American Economic Review, Papers and Proceedings*, pp. 197- 203

STIGLITZ, Joseph E. (1990): Peer Monitoring and Credit Markets, *The World Bank Economic Review*, Vol.4, pp. 351-366

STIGLITZ, Joseph E. (1991) Government, Financial Markets, and Economic Development, *NBER Working Paper No. 3669*, Cambridge, Mass.

STIGLITZ, Joseph E. (1991a): Financial Markets and Development, mimeo, Stanford

STIGLITZ, Joseph E.; WEISS, Andrew (1981): Credit Rationing in Markets with Imperfect Information, *American Economic Review*, Vol. 71, pp. 393-410

STIGLITZ, Joseph E.; WEISS, Andrew (1983): Incentive Effects of Terminations: Applications to the Credit and Labor Markets, *American Economic Review*, Vol. 73, pp. 912-927

TOKMAN, Victor E. (1978): An Exploration into the Nature of Informal-Formal Sector Relationships, *World Development*, Vol. 6, pp. 1065-1075

TYRELL, Marcel (1990): Der Ansatz der Ohio State University zur Bewertung und Gestaltung ländlicher Finanzsysteme, mimeo, Trier: Universität Trier

U TUN WAI (1977): A Revisit to Interest Rates Outside the Organized Money Markets of Underdeveloped Countries, *Banca Nazionale del Lavoro Quarterly Review*, Vol. 122, pp. 291-312

VILLANUEVA, Delano; MIRAKHOR, Abbas (1990): Strategies for Financial Reforms. Interest Rate Policies, Stabilization, and Bank Supervision in Developing Countries, *International Monetary Fund Staff Papers*, Vol. 37, pp. 509-536

VIRMANI, Arvind (1982): The Nature of Credit Markets in Developing Countries, A Framework for Policy Analysis, *World Bank Staff Working Paper No. 524*, Washington, D.C.: World Bank

VOGEL, Robert C. (1984): Savings Mobilization: The Forgotten Half of Rural Finance, in: Adams, D.W.; Graham, D.H.; Von Pischke, J.D. (eds.): *Undermining Rural Development with Cheap Credit*, Boulder: Westview Press, pp. 248-265

VOGEL, Robert C. (1988): The Role of Groups, Credit Unions and Other Cooperatives in Rural Lending, Washington, D.C.: World Bank

VON PISCHKE, J. D. (1988): Risk: The Neglected Dimension in Rural Credit Projects, in: *Fourth Technical Consultation on the Scheme for Agricultural Credit Development*, Rome: FAO, pp. 26-29

VON PISCHKE, J. D. (1991): *Finance at the Frontier: Debt Capacity and the Role of Credit in the Private Economy. EDI Development Studies*, Washington, D.C.: World Bank

VON PISCHKE, J. D. (1992): ROSCAs: State-of-the-Art Financial Intermediation, in: Adams, D. W.; Fitchett D. A. (eds.): *Informal*

Finance in Low-Income Countries, Boulder: Westview Press, pp. 325-335

VON PISCHKE, J. D.; ADAMS, Dale W.; DONALD, Gordon (eds.) (1983): *Rural Financial Markets in Developing Countries,* Baltimore/London: Johns Hopkins University Press

WEBSTER, Leila (1990): Fifteen Years of World Bank Lending for Small and Medium Enterprises, Washington, D.C.: World Bank; also in: *Small Enterprises Development,* Vol. 1, pp. 17-25

WEISBROD, Burton A. (1988): *The Nonprofit Economy,* Cambridge, Mass.: Harvard University Press

WIELAND, Robert C. (1988): A Summary of Case Studies of Group Lending and Cooperative Finance in LDCs, Washington, D.C: World Bank

WIGGINS, Steve; ROGALY, Ben (1989): Providing Rural Credit in Southern India: A Comparison of Commercial Banks and Cooperatives, *Public Administration and Development,* Vol. 9, pp. 215-232

WILLIAMSON, Oliver E. (1985): *The Economic Institutions of Capitalism: Firms, Markets, Relational Contracting,* New York: Free Press

WOLF, Bernhard (1984): *Zur Bedeutung der finanziellen Infrastruktur in Entwicklungsländern,* Berlin: Duncker & Humblot

WORLD COUNCIL OF CREDIT UNIONS (1988): Improving Financial Services in Rural Areas - The Credit Union Experience and Impact, in: *Fourth Technical Consultation on the Scheme for Agricultural Credit Development,* Rome: FAO, pp. 37-40

WORLD BANK (1983): Review of Financial Sector Work, Washington, D.C.: World Bank

WORLD BANK (1985): Review of Financial Sector Work, Washington, D.C.: World Bank Industry Department, Financial Development Unit

WORLD BANK (1989): Report of the Task Force on Financial Sector Operations (draft), Washington, D.C.: World Bank

WORLD BANK (1989a): *World Development Report*, Washington, D.C.: World Bank

ZEITINGER, Claus-Peter; SCHMIDT, Reinhard H. (1984): Kreditgarantiefonds - einige Überlegungen zu diesem Kreditfinanzierungsinstrument, Frankfurt(Main): Interdisziplinäre Projekt Consult

ABOUT THE BOOK AND AUTHORS

The authors of this timely analysis compare the different ways in which financial services in developing countries are provided to poor target groups largely cut off from formal financial systems: small and micro-scale business, small farmers, and women. They argue that building sustainable and target group-oriented financial institutions is important and feasible, and that such building is likely to have greater development impact than the channeling of external funds to poor target groups.

Yet the provision of financial services to the poor as well as institution-building efforts are likely to run into severe information and incentive problems. How these problems can be addressed and overcome is central to the authors' analysis. Drawing extensively on the conceptual tools of the new economics of information and institutions, Krahnen and Schmidt examine real-world cases of institution building. They consider formal and informal financial institutions, in particular group lending, rotating savings and credit associations (RoSCAs), and financial cooperatives, and demonstrate how information and institution economics can be put into practice.

Development Finance as Institution Building has far-reaching implications for development policy and the design of aid programs. It is crucial reading for development specialists, policymakers, and scholars of development finance and international banking.

This study has been prepared on behalf and with the support of the International Labour Office (ILO). It forms part of a program that explores the links between finance and poverty reduction.

Jan Pieter Krahnen is professor of finance at the University of Giessen, Germany. **Reinhard H. Schmidt** holds the Wilhelm-Merton Chair for International Business and Finance at the University of Frankfurt, Germany. Both authors are associates of IPC, the leading consulting firm in the field of development finance, and have served as consultants to several international donor agencies.

INDEX